Shamanic Reiki Drumming

"What I love about *Shamanic Reiki Drumming* is the beautiful way Fay integrates key healing elements into her practice. Connection to Spirit and being the 'hollow bone' are what allow and encourage healing to occur. Fay explains these basics very well and then guides the reader into deeper realms of drumming work, including its evocation of altered states to enter the Universal. Always present, and absolutely essential, are the constant currents of intuition and intention so the reader can access potent and lasting healing. You will enjoy this well-written and knowledgeable book."

— SHARON E. MARTIN, M.D., Ph.D., host of *Maximum Medicine* radio show and author of *Maximize Your Healing Power*

"Another beautifully written book by Fay Johnstone, full of insightful practices that bring reiki, drumming, and shamanism together. Crafted in a way we can all understand and benefit from, *Shamanic Reiki Drumming* serves as a guide for ourselves, our students, and our community. I am looking forward to working with many of these wonderful practices and sharing them with others. Thank you, Fay, for your inspiration."

— LORNA McLEAN, reiki master teacher and holistic practitioner

Shamanic
Reiki
Drumming

Intuitive HEALING with SOUND and VIBRATION

Fay Johnstone

 FINDHORN PRESS

Findhorn Press
One Park Street
Rochester, Vermont 05767
www.findhornpress.com

Text stock is SFI certified

Findhorn Press is a division of Inner Traditions International

Disclaimer
The information in this book is given in good faith and is neither intended to diagnose
any physical or mental condition nor to serve as a substitute for informed medical advice
or care. Please contact your health professional for medical advice and treatment. Neither
author nor publisher can be held liable by any person for any loss or damage whatsoever
which may arise from the use of this book or any of the information therein.

Cataloging-in-Publication data for this title is available from the Library of Congress

ISBN 978-1-64411-884-9 (print)
ISBN 978-1-64411-885-6 (ebook)

Printed and bound in the United States by Lake Book Manufacturing, LLC
The text stock is SFI certified. The Sustainable Forestry Initiative® program
promotes sustainable forest management.

10 9 8 7 6 5 4 3 2 1

Edited by Jacqui Lewis
Illustrations by Keri Manning-Dedman
Text design and layout by Damian Keenan
This book was typeset in Adobe Garamond Pro, Calluna Sans, with Daikon and
ITC Century Book Condensed used as display typefaces.

To send correspondence to the author of this book, mail a first-class letter to the
author c/o Inner Traditions • Bear & Company, One Park Street, Rochester,
VT 05767, and we will forward the communication, or contact the author directly at
www.fayjohnstone.com.

Contents

⌒

Appendix

Foreword

The drum: an eternal calling of a heartbeat through time. The drum: creation's consort; opener of pathways of communication through the realms; caller of the beings of the many worlds; synchronizer of body with spirit; steady, sturdy guardian of the soul. All of these things have I found the drum to be. All of these I have found through listening to the drum and seeing where its pulse will take me.

I have always been moved by the stories of how Tibetan lamas come to be found in their new incarnations. It is through the recognition and recalling of the instruments of a previous lifetime's craft that these compassionate souls are reunited with a spiritual calling that threads through time. How beautiful is that? Well, I can't lay claim to such a noble calling, but in lieu of the pull of a shamanic operator I feel the same way about the drum. Seeing shamanic instruments in museums as a child, my mind would immediately jump with visions of the spirit animals revealed by their skins. My imagination would plunge me into peaceful trance scenes, edgy in their atmospheres of power and richness. I also recall once, as a teenager in an Irish pub, somewhere in Leeds, feeling hypnotized by the pulse of a bodhrán, taken again into a parallel scene of drums beating, worlds opening, keying into a scene on Celtic lands of not so long ago. Then, I remember as a young adult being stranded in Greece for a while after missing the plane back from Crete. It was years later that, following the instruction of my drum, I would find my twenty-year-old soul part standing angrily at the docks with arms folded, demanding to know why I had left. I consciously clocked that of course a part of my soul would want to stay there. Crete is the island of Ariadne, the one who beats the frame drum for Theseus deep in the labyrinth with the Minotaur, to guide him out of the maze and safely back into the arms of life again. For some of us the drum and its mysteries are never forgotten.

I imagine that, as you've picked up a book that speaks of the rhythms of the drum, you may also be one of those people for whom the drum is never forgotten. I imagine you may be picking up this book as someone who has worked a little (or lots) with reiki or someone who works with the drum and is looking to understand a little more about the reiki and drum bridge that Fay Johnstone will walk you skilfully across.

For myself personally, I know that without being reunited with the drum in this lifetime, there are places that would never have been unlocked in my timeless soul. Perhaps you will be looking to unlock these places within yourself too.

I remember in 2006, returning from Findhorn where I had gone to live with my son and daughter, back to Fife to begin to teach shamanism on the land where my children had been born. On return, the most immense spiritual opening happened to me through the land of Fife. This left me stripped of energy. It was as if I had been taken back to a simpler version of myself for a rebuild. The way out of this living death was slow and it demanded a lot of patience. I had to keep very still. I couldn't be around negativity and I couldn't listen to talk that wasn't positive and life-affirming. I wondered what I could do to help this process. The answer came to me in a flash: "reiki".

I spent a year and a half undergoing reiki training from Level 1 right through to teacher level with my reiki teacher Claudia Duncan and a couple of other reiki practitioners-to-be. Reiki took me to a place of resourcing, kindness and listening that was just what my body and soul needed. It is my go-to whenever I start to feel myself coming out of balance. The nights that I still spend to this very day with the reiki guides and Usui's practice are some of my most favourite benevolent and loving spaces. Unlike Fay, I have never taught reiki, I simply have it always there. Despite knowing Fay through shamanic work, it was reiki that called us together in the lockdown reiki group of five that Fay speaks about in the later chapters of this book.

It is a delight to read these pages scribed by Fay that lead you and me, the readers, into the practice of reiki through the rhythms of the drum. What can I say that will give you some indication of the wonderful journey that you have in store?

In *Shamanic Reiki Drumming* Fay introduces you to the drum through her experience of it as a friend, helper and cosmic companion on her life's path. She shows how the practice of creative shamanism has assisted her own reiki practice to open up in ways that give it wider scope and a contemporary playfulness. In the opening chapters, Fay takes you through the experiences of her first encounters with the drum and goes on to carefully chart its appearance in the wealth of spiritual traditions that have evolved through time. This gives you an honest appreciation of some of what the drum will be for you, and important context and grounding with this living instrument. By the time the book opens to chart the way ahead, you can feel a readiness to explore the relationship further. And that is in fact just what Fay will do for you – she will help you to build a deep and lasting relationship with this magical instrument! Fay guides you through a process where you can, step by step, build a relationship with your drum and weave it with your reiki practice.

The drum and the practice of shamanism are detailed over several pages. Finding a drum, taking care of a drum, the way of holding and working with a drum are described to you in such a careful and considerate way. Fay leads you through the preparation for picking up and playing the drum so that by the time you are working with your drum a caring and sacred relationship will have developed. Through the telling of stories and anecdotes of her own personal experiences, a light-hearted tone trills you along. Fay is an expert guide, thorough and exact in laying down foundations and steps. You will find yourself in the hands of an incredible instructor and clear conveyor of tips and stages.

Fay guides you through a practice of drumming with reiki symbols and how this can support healing of individuals and environments. The expansion the drum enables is relayed with ease. In Fay's capable hands you will be guided through the practices of journeying, holding ceremony and connecting with guides as a part of the reiki practice, all with careful safety guidelines for starting out on an expansive practice.

The power of this book is really in its ability to hold the practical and mystical side of the drum and reiki side by side. This can only enable the reader looking to find inspiration for ways of working, to blend and find the same side-by-side development of practicality and mysticism with their own *Shamanic Reiki Drumming* practice.

This book is a blessing and a door opening wide to anyone who is curious to begin to explore and safely try out the practices in this book. Lots of the practices are suitable for beginner level. It offers a wide breadth of opportunities to work with reiki drumming, ranging from synchronization of self and environment to journeying for guidance, gentle house clearing and balancing, and beginning to hold reiki drumming circles. It is a valuable resource and manual for anyone with a reiki and shamanism background to learn how to begin to put the practices together through the drum. It is a significant and important springboard book for those who will inevitably be led deeper on the path of shamanic education through the rhythms of the reiki drum.

— **Carol Day**, founder of Creative Earth Ensemble and author of *Shamanic Dreaming*

The Beat Starts Here
Reiki, the Drum, and Me

◎ ◎ ◎ ◎

The very first time I picked up a hand-held drum and felt the beat of that ancient sound throughout my being, my life shifted. This simple act opened up a new reality for me; a world that had always been there but was now so easy to access, and in full technicolour, was begging me to dive in and explore. It was impossible to ignore.

The beat of the drum had called me home, home to a vivid place of imagination and rich with creative possibility. A new reality full of potential that seemed to ask, "What if?" and question "What is?". A place whose door I had previously closed had now been burst wide open by the rhythmic beat and vibration of the drum I held between my hands. I felt myself easily able to slip from the confines of my reality into this new and exciting place. My world had shifted, expanded and now had a new angle; it felt full of hope, alternative options and support.

That was in 2009 when, over a weekend training with Sarah Gregg, I was presented with a synthetic Remo buffalo drum and shown various different healing practices as part of the reiki drum technique.

Despite this technique being relatively new in the UK at the time, I felt like holding the drum and connecting with the frequency of the universe was something that my body and soul had been doing for ever, as if the sound of the drum spoke deeply to an ancient cellular memory held deeply in my being.

Since that moment, the drum, like my reiki practice, has been part of my life. That weekend opened up such a box of treasures, or can of worms really, and left me with so many questions that slowly, over the years, I have been shown answers to through deepening my shamanic practice. Meeting the drum in this way, with reiki as my silent blanket of comfort and support, led me to seek out shamanic teachers and drumming circles to help me to navigate the worlds that the drum had revealed to me, meet spirit guides, heal deep wounds and learn further ways that the drum works through us to heal and reveal our truth.

A reiki teacher once asked me, "What has the drum got to do with reiki?" in a highly disapproving manner. If you are a reiki purist, of course this book is not for you. Reiki is by its very nature a simple practice, easy to learn and use, without the need for complex training or tools; that is its beauty and also what makes it so versatile as a healing modality. As reiki practitioners we often say that we are the channel for reiki energy, and how this energy channels through us and how we express this and are guided to work with it is unique to each individual. As it flows through us or from us, it changes us and guides us. Some reiki practitioners place their hands on someone's body to heal, some work with their hands placed a few inches above the body in the energy field, others sit miles away in meditation and connect energetically. Some are guided to work with crystals and reiki, and others, like myself, work with plant medicines, sound, or even movement. Whether it be the drum, a crystal bowl, the tone of your voice or a tuning fork, sound frequency merges with the frequency of reiki to shift the energetic frequency to enable healing.

You could also ask the question, "What has reiki go to do with drumming?" The drum, in the sense that I am referring to working with it in these pages, goes beyond it being a simple musical instrument; rather, it is a shamanic tool, one of many that facilitate connection with the spirit worlds in shamanic healing practice. This will be covered in more detail in these pages. Personally I have found that, having been attuned to reiki for over twenty years, I cannot turn it off. Whenever I pick up my drum to work in a shamanic way, reiki will flow through me and the drum to where it is needed. It therefore feels more authentic to share with my clients and readers that reiki is involved. I refer to this practice as shamanic reiki. I cannot separate the two and the two enhance each other, as I will explain later.

Together with the benefits of reiki and all the spiritual connection and expansion that shamanic practice can bring, the drum is also a creator of sound waves. Sound therapy brings its own unique benefits to the healing process for mind, body and spirit. It is this trio of modalities – reiki, shamanism and sound therapy – that create the profound and potent possibilities for healing that occur when reiki practitioners pick up their drums.

The drum is a magical and ancient tool. What follows in these pages are a collection of my favourite ways to work with the drum and reiki, both for your personal growth and development and for enhancing client treatments or working in groups of practitioners. I will also be introducing you to shamanic practice and how it fits seamlessly with reiki. There's also a whole chapter dedicated to connecting with the natural world for healing and in ceremony, my favourite way to work with the drum. As well as the practical material I also wanted to share stories of the drum, so that the beat of the drum could help you sing your truth, take you on adventures and call you home.

The instigator for this book was a vivid dream that I experienced early in 2022 in which I spoke at length and in great detail to one of my teachers, Carol Day. In the dream and with great excitement I told Carol all about my new book combining reiki practice and the drum. Such was the vibrancy and energy that held the dream that when I woke up in the morning, it was still with me in my heart. On opening my eyes I felt a shift, like another layer of my blinkers had been lifted and I could see through the veil more clearly. To my amusement, when I told my husband about the new book, he simply replied: "Haven't you written a book about that yet?"

Reiki and the drum have been part of my practice for over fourteen years, and now feels like the right time to share my stories with you. The drum has gifted me with enormous creativity, expansion and insight. If the energy behind this book can help me see more clearly and receive what is already there, then my hope is that it can do so for you too. You will feel for yourself – or perhaps already know – the expansive power that the drum carries as it shifts your frequency into harmony with your authentic nature. May you find your own rhythm with this exciting path and start dancing from your heart to the beat of your own drum.

1

Reiki and Shamanism

⊚ ⊚ ⊚ ⊚

I'm beginning this book with a few simple definitions of reiki and shamanism so we start off this journey together with a mutual understanding. Though I must admit that it pains me to do so, since the moment we put something in a box by defining it and declaring it so, we limit its power. That is in fact the very opposite of my intention. So please view this chapter with curiosity, asking for yourself: how can reiki healing and the innate practice of shamanism combine? What makes shamanic practices shamanism and reiki healing reiki? Where does your reiki practice end and your shamanic practice with the drum begin? The edges are blurry. Perhaps the two have more in common than you think?

Let's Start with Reiki

Given the title of this book, it's most likely that you are already a practitioner of reiki or have a keen interest in energy healing, and therefore it may feel unnecessary to go over the ins and outs of reiki in too much detail. Plus, there are numerous books, guides, manuals and YouTube videos that detail, often very well, the specifics of reiki practice, its techniques and origins.

You might be familiar with the standard description of reiki as a system of healing that works with universal life energy for the highest good, which originated in Japan with Dr Mikao Usui and is passed down, via a lineage of masters and practitioners, through an attunement process.

However, no matter at what stage you are on your reiki journey, you will also have formed your own ideas about reiki as the energy flows through you. The more we practise reiki, the more we align with the very essence of who we are. This shifts our perception of reiki (and ourselves) and guides us on our own unique path of healing and self-discovery. As you practice reiki, either with self-practice or with friends, family, pets and clients, the more experience you gain of connecting with the energy and the deeper insight you receive. This experience transforms the way you practise reiki and expands your sense of who you truly are as an energetic being. You naturally gravitate towards practices that feel right for you and leave aside those techniques and meditations that don't feel useful in your practice. You may even be guided intuitively to create your own practices and healing processes.

Reiki channels through (or perhaps from) the practitioner and is activated by intention. The most common technique is the laying on of hands, with a light touch and with set hand positions. However, many practitioners are guided by intuition and many other ways of sending reiki healing exist, such as beaming reiki without touching through the hands, with the eyes, with the breath, with the use of symbols, the voice or even movement – and of course, as we will focus on in these pages, the drum.

Rather than regurgitate the usual reiki descriptives, I invite you to sit for a moment with your hands together in *gassho* (prayer position) and reflect on your reiki journey.

SELF-REFLECTION **You and Your Reiki Path**

- What is reiki to you?
- Reiki is an intelligent energy and works for the highest good; it can do no harm – but where does it come from?
- How do you know that reiki is flowing?
- What experiences with reiki have impacted you the most?
- What is nudging you to connect with the drum?

Introduction to Shamanism

Shamanism is one of the oldest forms of spirituality in the world and some even call the practice an instinctive connection to our true nature. The very thought of it feels exciting to many of us, as it links us to an innate way of connecting with the world that Western culture has lost and yet longs for. Today there are many books that cover shamanism, its techniques and practices in detail, so I'm just going to provide a brief overview of my understanding from which you can develop your own.

Shamanism is an innate creative practice in which we embody and communicate with the vibratory consciousness that runs throughout the universe; that is nature, that is us! We experience and shape the very creative force that connects and creates all things. In shamanic practice, the shaman (or practitioner) works with helping spirits in order to navigate other worlds and dimensions to bring about healing or receive guidance. Shamanism works in harmony with the spirit of all things and calls upon the forces of nature for healing in order to maintain the balance in the community. Shamanic cultures have an animistic belief that there is spirit in everything: trees, mountains, animals, plants, humans, bodies of water, the weather, and so on. This interconnectivity with all of life creates a sense of magic and connection that speaks to us at soul level. Spirit (or in reiki practice we might say energy) is in everything and infuses life.

We might also think of this as everything having a consciousness. Interestingly, many consider Shinto or "Way of the Gods", the indigenous religion of Japan (where reiki originated) to be a form of animism because of the similarities they share. Shintoism has many gods (sacred and divine beings or things that inspire a sense of awe), known as kami; these include mountains, bodies of water, landscape, ancestors, souls of the dead, weather and other natural elements. I find this link to reiki's origins helps explain the mindset of both the reiki practitioner and the shaman. It also helps us reiki practitioners connect with the shamanic nature that we have within ourselves.

When you think about shamanic cultures, you might instantly think of indigenous tribes like those of South America, Africa and Siberia. The concept of a wise elder or village medicine man or woman might also come to mind. Many of these indigenous people do still honour their shamanic lineages with customs, spirit guides and rituals that have been handed down from generation to generation. You may be drawn to a specific shamanic lineage like Huichol or Toltec from Mexico, Q'ero from the Peruvian Andes, Shipibo of the Amazon, or Navajo (Diné) from the south-western United States, for example; each of these has its own spirit guides, tools, and traditions.

Though not as well-known as other shamanic traditions, there is a long history of shamanism in Japan. Japanese shamen were traditionally blind women and they acted as a conduit for the voices and powers of the kami and other spirits. What remains of this tradition are the contemporary miko or shrine maidens. These young women are seen at Shinto shrines, where they assist with shrine functions, perform ceremonial dances and offer *omikuji* fortune-telling. If you are interested in finding out more about the history of shamanic practices of Japan, *The Catalpa Bow* provides essential reading. Written by a British scholar who spent time living in Japan, this book is a fascinating account of Shinto and shamanism. It shares both an academic and a hands-on point of view from her own experience of participating in many of the rituals and practices.

I believe that in the Western world, our ancestors were shamen too. The traditional lineages of medicine people in the West have been lost and replaced by doctors, vets, priests, dowsers, mediums, philosophers, writers, artists, storytellers, leaders, herbalists, politicians, counsellors, and so on. This is why we now have shamanic practitioners who have trained in core techniques based on those practised throughout the world by indigenous cultures. Contemporary practitioners are reigniting the culture that brings alive this innate way of being. We are remembering once more that we are conscious co-creators. This is not a New Age concept, it's more like a Stone Age practice; it was initiated by our ancient ancestors, as is possibly evident from the depictions of it in the Paleolithic cave art that we can still see around the world today. It is theorised that the humanoids painted on cave walls in areas like the Kimberley in Australia, Kondoa in Tanzania and Lascaux in France are demonstrating early shamanic practice and connection to the spirit world. The power of all of these shamanic practices lies in the connection that the shaman (or practitioner) has with their team of helping spirits. It's only by fostering this relationship and listening deeply that the shaman can be guided to bring back the knowledge or healing that is needed. In order to meet with the helping spirits, a shamanic practitioner will enter into an altered state and travel to non-ordinary realities; this key process is known as the shamanic journey and will be discussed in more detail in subsequent chapters.

There are numerous well-researched books available that share different aspects of shamanism in much more detail than I can here. This is simply intended to introduce you to the concept, so that we have an understanding and can move forward together in this book. Since the practice of shamanism is not a spectator sport, rather a felt and embodied experience, I encourage you to research and practise whichever techniques or traditions call to you. Over time, as you develop a trusting relationship with your guides, you will most certainly be led to teachers, books and courses that shape your understanding, offer you the healing you need and provide you with the knowledge that you require for your own path.

What Is Shamanic Reiki?

Throughout this book you may find me referring to shamanic reiki. Quite simply, this term refers to the Japanese healing energy technique of reiki combined with shamanism. The combination of the two modalities is activated by the intention to bring about guidance and healing. Both reiki and shamanism work with the field of unified energy that encompasses us all and can transcend time and space. For many who practise it, reiki is a spiritual path, and shamanism too becomes a way of life for those who follow its path. Each modality has a great respect for all living things and as the practice of each evolves so too does the practitioner's intuition, self-awareness, ability to shift into an altered state and relationship with spirit allies.

As a reiki practitioner, I don't believe that we can "turn off" our connection to reiki energy. Therefore, when reiki practitioners begin to journey with the drum or work with other shamanic techniques, we always remain connected to reiki. Whatever shamanic path we experience, we walk it with reiki flowing through us, supporting us with its high-vibrational frequency of love and nurture. It feels more authentic for me to refer to this path as shamanic reiki, rather than simply shamanism.

Shamanic Reiki – How Does It All Combine Together?

For me, shamanism is a natural extension of, and accompaniment to, my reiki practice. Both shamanism and reiki are:

- Focused on self-healing – The more we are able to bring compassion and understanding to our own healing, the more we come into alignment with our true self and are able to hold a clear space to help others.
- Activated by intention – Our intention for healing is the focus and the driver of the transformation.
- Spirit-led – As we practise we remain open to the nudge of spirit helpers during our work and follow guidance and information that is revealed to us.
- Intuitive – When I practise shamanic reiki, I don't follow the suggested hand positions of traditional reiki practice; rather it is a case of moving to areas that I am intuitively drawn to or feel guided to work on. The more you practise in this way, the more you will start to trust your special senses and the stronger they will become.

- More interactive – Often a traditional reiki treatment can seem quite passive. The client shows up and after a brief chat to establish what they wish to focus on, they lie down on the couch and often fall asleep as they receive healing. In contrast, I experience shamanic reiki treatments to be more dynamic and involve the client's participation in a more proactive way. Treatments may include a discussion with your client, guided visualization, or client participation during the treatment. If you are using the drum there is an especially dynamic and transformative, active element to the healing.
- Empowering for the client – A client will be directly involved with their own healing, not just receiving; this deepens your relationship with your client and empathy for them, which in turn leads to deeper healing sessions and the potential for powerful transformation.
- Working in harmony with nature – An essential quality in shamanic reiki is to work in reverence with the spirit in all things and especially the natural world.
- Open to creativity and versatility – there is no wrong way. Healing and transformation are fuelled by intention and guided by spirit helpers and reiki.
- Able to treat clients, situations, places in nature or animals in person, over a distance, in the past, future, or present moment.

Working with shamanic reiki will:

- Bring you into alignment with your true nature and gifts.
- Strengthen your relationship with your guides and your intuition.
- Revitalize your relationship with the living world around you: the elements, plants, birds, animals, weather, seasons, cycles of the moon and landscape, for example.
- Open up your physical and intuitive senses to a broader way of connecting to and practising reiki.
- Strengthen your connection to / understanding of reiki energy.
- Help you embody a broader sense of wholeness and harmony.
- Provide you with a new healing tool, both for personal practice and to expand your client work.

- Bring different clients to your practice who are interested in the drum and shamanism.

What Is Reiki Drum?

This shamanic reiki technique combines the use of a hand-held drum with the reiki symbols and mantras learned at reiki Level 2 to introduce reiki into a client's energy field. The beat of the drum reminds the energy field of its optimal vibration, its unique frequency. This can help bring about homeostasis in the body and induce a feeling of deep relaxation, releasing deep-seated tension. Practitioners also use the drum to enter the journey state to obtain information and guidance to assist the client. Various techniques are used when combining reiki and the drum; practitioners may drum reiki symbols over the client's body during a session, or they may work with the drum and the symbols with a different focus.

Note: reiki drumming is a trademarked therapy that uses the drum and reiki and was developed by Michael Arthur Baird in 1999. The technique was brought to the UK by Sarah Gregg, which is how I learned it, in 2009. Since then I have studied creative shamanism and added other shamanic techniques to my reiki practice, hence the broader term applied in this book: shamanic reiki.

Non-ordinary Reality and the Journey

It is said that the shaman walks with one foot in the spirit world and one in this reality. The shaman has to leave the everyday life behind and walk between worlds into non-ordinary reality to access power, energy and wisdom that can help the community or client. Just like a reiki practitioner, the shaman is a hollow bone, a conduit for energy and information. The shaman's journey is a conscious daydream fuelled by your imagination and experience. The most common way in the West for you to practise this way of journeying is through the repetitive beat of the drum. Practising this way of journeying and connecting to other worlds is like working a muscle that builds strength and stamina. The more you practise, the deeper your connections and the more you experience and receive. The more open and curious you are in the journey state, the more information you can gain to bring back to help your clients. I will be guiding you through the journey process in a later chapter as it's an essential technique to develop your relationship with guides and helpers who will bring their wisdom to your practice.

TAKE ACTION Light a Candle for Your Ancestors

Consider those who have gone before you. It's likely that each of us has ancestors who were at least familiar with shamanic practices and healing ways, or were maybe practising themselves and living a life that was interwoven with the spirits of the land and nature. This ancient knowledge and connectedness are within your DNA.

Choose a place either outside in a special place in nature or in your reiki space at home. Invite reiki to flow in the way that you have been taught. Light a candle here for your ancestors, to honour the lives they led, the wisdom that they shared and all the love and blessings that they hold for you.

You may wish to say a prayer or simply light the candle in their memory. Tell them that you wish to reach out to them and ask that they help you unlock the knowing within you and remember all the ancient wisdom that is yours to know. Spend ten minutes beaming reiki to your ancestors (using the reiki 2 distance/connection symbol) and then finish your practice by offering your thanks. Note down any reflections or memories that have surfaced.

Shamanic Techniques

The shaman walks between the worlds and opens up to the invisible energies that exist there. Like reiki practitioners, a shaman's role is to help clients access the power within and bring their vibration back into harmony with the universal vibration. I sometimes think of this as pressing the reset button, untangling a client from their negative past experiences, thought patterns, trauma or stuck energy that is not part of the client's true original story. This restores wholeness and flow, bringing a client back into balance with their true and divine nature.

You may already be familiar with shamanic techniques such as:

- Extractions or removal of intrusions: taking away energy that does not belong to the client.
- Cutting cords: releasing the client from energetic attachments that still connect the client to a person, place, event, object and are not helping.

- Soul restoration: restoring fragments of the soul that may have been misplaced, forgotten about, lost or abandoned.
- Power retrieval: bringing back an aspect of a client's power in the form of an animal, for example.
- Healing ancestral patterns.
- Psychopomp: helping souls who have got stuck in this reality to cross over into the light.
- Assisting with death and transition.
- Healing hexes, breaking spells and lifting curses.
- Land healing.
- Transfiguration: a shape-shifting process of experiencing your light and radiating it out into the world to create positive change.

Just like reiki practitioners, a shamanic practitioner may focus on national and global situations as well as personal healing for clients and themselves.

Your Shamanic Nature

We all have an innate shamanic nature that is our intuitive way of being in the world, and I believe that, as we practise reiki, it brings this authentic nature out of us and helps us to release the barriers that have been preventing us from stepping into our true self. The shaman is your essential nature, the part of you that knows, intuits and shines as the flow of power that connects with and becomes the consciousness of the universe.

SELF-REFLECTION Reiki, Shamanism, the Drum, and You

Consider the following:
- What is your experience of reiki and shamanism or working with the drum so far?
- How do you access your knowing?
- How do you envisage working with the drum in your reiki practice?
- If you could combine the above into one specific intention for this book, what would that be?

2

Sound and Symbols

This chapter explores the healing medicine of sound, different shamanic tools, instruments and of course the drum. I've also included a recap of the reiki 2 symbols as these are a useful accompaniment to your reiki drum treatments and help focus different aspects of the energy for specific healing.

> *I still have a tear in my throat.*
>
> *The silent scream that was never heard except by the universe inside me.*
>
> *It warped the fabric of time and shifted my harmony into a tune that played familiar notes with a sad, angry sound that felt wrong and took away the ability to remember what feels right.*

Healing with Sound

Like reiki, sound has a frequency; it is a travelling vibration. In fact, everything is vibrating and each of us has a specific frequency that helps us maintain optimum health and well-being. We are a very clever orchestra that creates a unique sound. When something happens that shocks or alters this frequency, causing a part of the body to vibrate in a different way, this upsets our internal orchestra, which over time can cause dis-ease. If for example we suffer unresolved trauma in our childhood, it can cause our frequency to misalign and vibrate in a way that is not our true resonance, which might cause our health to suffer.

Over time our bodies can become stuck playing songs that are not their own and it's these negative patterns that reiki and sound can help to shift. When you work with your drum and reiki, your aim is to restore the music (the unique vibration) of yourself or your client and bring you, or them, back to health and wholeness.

You may be familiar with Dr Masaru Emoto's research into water. His book *The Hidden Messages in Water* demonstrates the effect that sound has on water molecules. With beautiful imagery, he shows us that different sounds change the physical structure of water. The reason why this is an important discovery is because over 60 per cent of our bodies are water. This means that the sounds that go on around us (and through us) are physically shaping our structure – for better or for worse. We are indeed very susceptible to sound.

Often when people think of sound healing, they think of soothing music. Yes, sound can be very relaxing and music such as binaural beats has been developed to shift brainwaves for this purpose. However, there is a difference between sound and music, which it can be useful to clarify for yourself so that you can share this with clients. Beyoncé, Mozart: they make what we call music. Whereas leaves rustling, doors slamming, running water and babies crying are examples of sounds.

With your drum you will be creating sound, beating a frequency and a rhythm to help bring a client into alignment with their unique resonance; you won't necessarily be creating music. The beat that you might be playing is often very repetitive rather than a catchy tune. Often when people hear that I work with the drums, they think that I am a drummer. I am not; I don't know how to play a drum kit. But I do know how to work with my drum and reiki and allow myself to be guided by the natural beats that I sense are flowing.

Shamanic Tools

In shamanic practice, the shaman also uses tools and instruments, but rather than for the purposes of sound therapy, they are tools to call to the spirit world. A shaman's tools help them access an altered state of being in order to travel to connect with helping beings and benevolent spirits. In the Western world, the most accessible tool for us is the hand-held drum or rattle. However, plant medicines, repetitive dance and other such practices may also be used.

Shamanic tools that help connect to the other dimensions include:

- The repetitive use of instruments such as the hand-held drum, rattles and bells or click sticks, clappers and digeridoos.
- Mirrors, costume and masks.
- Rhythmic dance, song and/or chanting.

- Psychoactive plants such as ayahuasca (a mix of Amazonian plants), mushrooms and peyote (cactus).
- Bee medicine.
- Earth, water, fire and air.
- Feathers, crystals, stones, flowers, plants, eggs, guinea pigs.
- Just about anything and everything – the power is not in the object or the technique but in the intention!

The Drum through the Ages

For thousands of years drumming has been a deep and sacred part of indigenous cultures across the world. When you pick up your drum, you too are connecting to this powerful legacy. From the Celts and Native Americans to Sami, Mongolians, North African and Arabic tribes, drumming has been an influential part of the culture, of great importance at weddings, funerals, harvest, initiations and other ceremonies.

The drum is one of the oldest known musical instruments. There is a shrine painting at Çatalhöyük in modern-day Turkey that shows human figures playing various percussion instruments including the frame drum. This is the earliest known depiction of the frame drum and is dated circa 5800 BCE.

This powerful spiritual tool is the simple frame drum made of animal hide. The wood of the drum carries the spirit of the tree that it is made from and may also represent the world tree or tree of life. The animal hide that covers the drum carries the spirit of the animal used, which might be reindeer, moose, cow, goat or others. The drum itself may also carry the intentions and energies of those who made it, the land where it was born, the phase of the moon during which it was created, together with any other materials that were used in its creation or decoration, such as plant dyes, feathers or stones.

Drums may be painted or dyed, or even carry symbols. In modern times we have created a vegan drum from synthetic materials. It has a constant sound, unaffected by the damp, which is very handy in the rain! Personally, I find my synthetic Remo drum to be a lifesaver when I'm caught outside in a downpour, which often happens in Scotland; the tone of the drum doesn't waver and never sounds flat. Some cultures associate the drum with the sun, others the moon, and their drums might be decorated accordingly.

The frame drum has a fascinating history stretching from prehistoric times to our present day. Traditionally the drummers were women and the drum was associated with the Goddess traditions, the oracle, prophecy, and wisdom. When I pick up my drum I feel that I too connect to this lineage of female drummers and weavers of wisdom. Over the millennia the drum has been seen as a symbol of connection, so much so that at certain stages in history it has even been banned, such is its power to unite and bring insight.

The drumbeat is an ancient signal to spirit and represents the inner pulse of all life. Your drum is the heartbeat of the universe, and it is also the link to your own heart! So look after it well and build a relationship with your drum – it is an extension of you! I feel this bond particularly strongly with the drum that I made ten years ago in Canada from hemlock wood and deerskin. I hear it singing to me in my sleep, as if it calls to me.

Drumming Inspiration from Japan

There are many varieties of traditional drum and percussion instruments found in Japan and records suggest drums have been in use there since the sixth century. A quick internet search will reveal links to the incredible sound created by drumming ensembles in impressive performances known as *kumi-daiko*, which we refer to in the West as *taiko*. It's hard not to be blown away by the sheer scale, size, and power of some of these drums and the skill and endurance that the performers must have to play them. The largest of all in an ensemble is the *ōdaiko* ("big taiko" in Japanese) and playing it looks like a real workout. These drums can be over 3.5m in diameter and, due to their size, may live permanently in a temple or shrine. Though historically these drums are not played with a healing intention, there is undoubtedly a transformative energy to the performances, sound, and rhythm. If you have never heard them before, then make it your task to do so – you are in for a treat.

The Science of the Drum

The drumbeat has various physical and physiological effects on the human body. Drumming creates sound waves; so the beat of the drum does not stop at the body, it enters the body as waves. This means it has great power to shift stagnant energy, release emotions and energy blockages and create change. The drumbeat shifts our brainwaves out of the beta state (concentration) so that the dormant parts awaken in alpha, theta or delta states. A brief drumming session can double alpha brain activity, which produces euphoria and a feeling of well-being. This helps us to feel calm and relaxed – you could call it a natural high.

Alpha is the rhythm of nature and is associated with euphoric or altered states such as meditation and shamanic journeys. Many say that the drumbeat brings us into deeper connection with Mother Earth and helps us connect with nature, since it helps us to operate at that frequency. I have certainly found this to be the case and it is one of the highlights of my practice and a constant source of inspiration for my path.

The drum engages both the right and the left brain and synchronizes both hemispheres, which helps produce a sense of clarity and heightened awareness. When the logical left hemisphere and the intuitive right hemisphere of your brain begin to pulsate together, your inner guidance system – or intuition – becomes stronger. This is highly beneficial in shamanic reiki practice and not only helps you increase your day-to-day trust in yourself but can also help you feel more confident when receiving intuitive guidance.

Listening to drum sounds regularly can have the same effect as drumming itself so, even when you can't play for yourself, you will experience similar benefits by listening to a drumming track.

It has been shown that drumming alters neuro-endocrine and immunological response in the body and facilitates deep relaxation. This helps reduce stress, anxiety, and tension and is also helpful when treating insomnia and asthma. The drum also helps us feel a sense of connectedness and can therefore help those feeling depressed, lonely or a sense of separation.

Research demonstrates that drumming can affect cortisol levels and blood pressure and increase the activity of natural killer cells in the body. It may also increase the production of endorphins, which helps with pain control and so may also be helpful in chronic pain management and in conditions such as arthritis.

The sound of drumming generates new neuronal connections in all parts of the brain. The more connections that can be made within the brain, the more integrated our experiences become. This leads to a deeper sense of self-awareness and self-acceptance, which helps us take responsibility for our own healing. I have also found that drum circles help to create a sense of connection and community, both to each other and to the Earth itself.

Drumming also appears to synchronize the lower areas of the brain (non-verbal) with the frontal cortex (language and reasoning). This integration produces feelings of insight and certainty.

For these reasons therapeutic drumming may be a powerful tool in helping retrain the brains of people who have some level of damage or impairment, such as with attention deficit disorder (ADD), after a stroke, or where there is neurological disease, such as Parkinson's.

Other studies have shown drumming's positive effect on patients with Alzheimer's and dementia, as they are able to follow rhythm even when other forms of communication have diminished.

Drumming feels like a natural accompaniment to reiki as both reduce stress, boost the immune system, help release trauma, and promote well-being. With the increase in popularity of sound healing therapies, more and more research is being published that supports their health claims and benefits. If you or a client suffer from a specific issue you may be interested to find out whether any targeted research has been conducted in that area. We are all unique and sound affects us all differently; there is no one rhythm that fixes every backache or heartbreak. It's the role of the practitioner and their drum to attune to the rhythm of the client and their unique circumstances and play the frequency that is needed – that is, their magic frequency.

Which Drums and Where to Get Them

I highly recommend getting hold of your own drum, or attending a workshop to make your own, so that you can practise as much as possible with the drum in all aspects of your life. It is great fun drumming in the garden or a favourite place in nature as well as in the treatment space. While you can practise the shamanic journey (which we will discuss more in the next chapter) by listening to a drumming recording, it's quite a different experience when you work with your own drum. I recommend practising both ways. You can always record yourself drumming a journey for yourself.

As with all spiritual tools, there are those that are factory-made and seem quite generic but are good value and a good place to start, and those that are handmade, unique and sometimes quite beautiful with a price tag to match, as well as everything in between. You will need to consider your budget and also what feels right for you.

Synthetic Drums

These are known these days as vegan drums and are a great starting point. I've had one of mine since 2009 and it's been soaked in the rain and through a firewalk and it's still going strong.

What you need to know about synthetic drums:

- They maintain their sound quality no matter what. The drum head is not affected by the cold or the damp. This means that you can play them in the rain, on cold damp mornings or on winter days. You can always trust in the sound.
- They are available in many sizes and styles – you can choose a drum that you hold at the back or at the side, or even an ocean drum that contains ball bearings and makes a sound like the sea. I have a 16-inch drum that creates deep tones and also a tiny 7-inch drum, which is convenient to travel with due to its small and packable size.
- They can be painted and personalized with acrylic paints.
- They are easy to obtain.
- They offer value for money and consistent-quality sound.

I recommend those that are produced by musical instrument producers rather than those produced by children's toy companies. For example, synthetic Remo buffalo drums are a great place to start and usually carry beautiful tones. If you have a local music store – ask them what they have.

Hide Drums

These drums are often handmade by a shamanic practitioner, so will be imbued with the energy of the maker as well as the energetic vibration of the animal whose hide has been used as the skin of the drum and of the tree whose wood has been used in the frame.

What you need to know about hide drums:

- They carry the spirit (energies) of the maker's intention, the animal and the plants or other materials that were used in their production.
- They are often made from deer, cow, buffalo or goatskin.

- They are unique, often beautiful, and can be tailored to a design of your choice with specific crystals or talismans included.
- They are sensitive to damp and cold, so will have poor sound quality unless heated by a fire/heater. This can make them unreliable if working outside or in damp conditions. They can also get easily damaged if they become too hot and dry.
- They are available only from specialist shamanic crafters, so may have limited availability and quality will vary widely – get a recommendation if possible.
- Prices and quality can vary and they can be expensive.

There are many handmade shamanic hide drums on sale via sites like eBay and Etsy, but these get very expensive – you have been warned!

I highly recommend making your own; it's a deep process that really connects you in a unique way to your drum. Look out for drum-making workshops in your area.

My life in a Drum

Late autumn during the hunting season, I was lucky enough to attend a drum-making workshop in my local area of Nova Scotia. The deerskin was found by a local shamanic practitioner; it was one of those that are discarded following a recreational kill by careless hunters out from the city looking for a thrill. My group had already been hard at work preparing the deerskin for use; we were certainly not going to let this beautiful skin go to waste and would honour it as best we could. Several frames had already been prepared by a local craftsman using wood from the trees in the area. I was drawn to a 12-sided frame made from hemlock wood. It was beautiful and felt just right for me that day.

I remember drawing around the frame and judging the size of hide required. After cutting out the size, I set to dying the hide. I treated the hide like I was tie-dying a t-shirt and tied the drum head with string as I immersed it in a deep basin full of black walnut infusion. After an hour of impatiently striding up and down watching the seconds go slowly by, I pulled out the hide, rinsed it off and untied the knots to see how the dye had taken. I was overwhelmed by the vision that was placed before me. On what was to become the drum head I could clearly see three deep-brown tree trunks with skeletal branches opening towards the centre of the hide on a cream background. The vision instinctively made me think of Africa and baobab trees. It was beautiful and totally unique. I was already astounded and the drum was not even halfway there!

What followed seemed like hours of torture! The strips of hide that I had cut to tie the hide to the drum were either so stiff and inflexible they would not bend and tighten or they were too thin and would break with any resistance. I wanted to pull the hide as taut as possible over the drum frame, yet the hide strips were resisting. To make matters worse, as the hide had dried it had also shrunk slightly, and the result was an irregular shape that did not easily stretch over the drum head. There was little extra to wrap around the back of the drum and secure it tightly. I had my work cut out here. In fact, creating my drum involved the help of many of those in my workshop, as I ran out of steam and patience pulling the unforgiving, tenacious strips of hide into position to make the drum fit onto the frame with the right amount of tension.

I gritted my teeth, I growled more than a hundred times and I swore at my drum as I pulled and stretched and knotted the hide together. When I had finally finished and created the drum, all I could do was to lie back and mutter fondly, "You little bastard," and so my drum was informally christened with her familiar name.

As I proudly held the completed drum for the first time together with the other workshop participants, I felt the power of this object. This drum contained all of me. All of my efforts, frustrations, excitement, hopes, dreams and disappointments were somehow represented in this object of hide and wood. It felt like the most personal object that I had ever created, it felt like it was part of me. I completely understood why we talk about "birthing a drum". I had just done that very thing! It wasn't just an object that I had created, it was an object that sang and resonated with my frequency and song.

That evening I drove home with the completed drum, totally spent from a weekend of focus and creation. I proudly placed my drum next to me at my bedside, not wanting to lose sight of this beautiful new being that seemed to be pulsing with life. As I slept I heard her singing to me with a distinctive beat that resonated deep within my bones. I heard her name calling to me in a language that I've never heard spoken in this time and place, and yet it spoke to me so clearly that it still rings in my heart. She told me her name and I understood that it was meant for me only, so Little Bastard is my term of endearment that not only speaks volumes but is easy to share.

A few years later I began a three-year shamanic training programme and as I was calling in a guide as a protector, a very familiar energy greeted me. First I met this guide several times as an African tribal warrior. It wasn't until later that I realized this man was a baobab tree and was my drum reaching out to protect me throughout my work and healing process. I felt truly blessed – and also a complete dunce for taking so long to catch on. But hey, spirit is timeless, it's only the ego that counts and competes.

I've learned now that this drum is so special to me, as a part of me, that it doesn't come to every event, workshop or healing. This drum is part of my unique journey with a distinctive frequency set for specific times, places and people. I keep listening for her beat, and know that she will nudge me by playing louder and louder until I listen and take action. Every time I reach for this special drum I understand that I am weaving part of my soul out into the web that unites us all, and I know that despite the drama it took to create, each part of the song is worth playing.

Drum Sizing and Sound

You can get any size that you wish or can find. Bear in mind the larger the drum diameter, the deeper the sound it carries and the more variation in tone you will experience.

Smaller drums that you hold by the rim (like a tambourine) can be very handy if you travel a lot; however, they don't have the depth of sound that you will experience with a larger diameter such as 14–18 inches.

During the drum-making workshop that I attended, another participant had selected a very large frame to create her drum. Over the weekend, the tension in the hide holding the drum in place had caused the drum to change in shape from a perfect circle to an oval. The end result was a drum that looked like a shield. The woman who created it was tiny and when she held it up in front of her it covered most of her torso. The protective energy of this drum radiated across the room; it was clear that this drum would shield her from harm. She left the workshop ten feet taller with confidence and certainty.

Holding a drum: Most larger drums that are used in shamanic reiki practice are held at the back with cord or strips of animal hide pulled tight, and are played with a drum beater with a hide or felt head or with the palm of your hand. Being able to hold the drum at the back gives you more flexibility than holding it by its frame, so bear this in mind when making your purchase. Many handcrafted drums will also have crystals, stones, feathers, carved wood or other sacred objects and talismans woven into the back; they can be tailored to your preference.

How a drum is fastened at the back is also very varied. I've seen shapes of trees, goddesses, dragons, spirit animals, five-pointed stars and crosses. However, no matter how beautiful these crafted pieces are, remember that the drum needs to be comfortable in your hand so that you can play it for as long as you need to without your hand getting chafed.

Frame drums are versatile; you don't have to stick to holding them at the back in the air and using your beater. For a more loving and nurturing heart connection you can cradle the drum in your non-dominant arm, hold it by your heart or balance the drum on your knee while seated. For more creativity and fun you can even play the drum freehand-style, sitting upright with your spine straight and placing it between your knees with the drum head slightly tilted towards you at an angle like a djembe drum. It can be played without the beater, just with your hands.

Drum beaters: Often drums come with their own beater with a soft padded end, but do check. You can make your own by selecting a piece of wood from nature, allowing it to fully dry and then covering one end with foam or rags and securing it with cord or animal hide. You don't have to use a beater; often I work just by using one or both hands to tap out a rhythm. This helps me feel more connected to the drum rhythm and creates a different feeling in the healing process. You can make a variety of different sounds with your hands, such as stroking the drum in a soft circular motion, tapping the edge with the pads of your two middle fingers, using the whole hand like a paw, using fingertips or tapping on the rim. Experiment and see what speaks to you as you play your drum.

As part of my plant spirit reiki practice I will often use a plant to create sound on my drum head. This creates a soft, gentle sound and also brings the spirit of the plant into the session.

Drum bags or carriers: If you will be travelling a lot with your drum or working outside, you may feel the need to protect it by purchasing a special padded and shaped drum bag or carrier. This is not necessary but can give you peace of mind as you know you'll be preventing damage. You will become very attached to your drums! Many producers also offer drum bags in sizes that match the drums they sell, so make sure you know the diameter of your drum. I've currently got six drums and not one single drum carrier; I seem to have managed so far with large shoulder bags and blankets to safely wrap them in. I'm sure a drum carrier will come to me when it is needed.

TAKE ACTION Rooting Yourself before You Drum

At the centre of the balls of the feet is a special point, an energetic gate often referred to in qigong or acupuncture practice as "bubbling spring." When you bring conscious awareness to this point with your feet on the ground and relax, a natural channel is activated and you will receive energy directly from the Earth. This nourishing energy can then move up the body through your receiving channels to nourish the legs and vital organs.

Before you drum, stand comfortably with your feet about hip-width apart, and soften your ankles, knees and hips. Invite your head, eyes, jaw, shoulders and back to relax. Roll your shoulders up, back and down to invite them to release tension. Drop your mind to your belly and breathe gently but deeply into this area. Soften and allow yourself to relax a little bit more with each exhalation. Allow your energetic roots to unfurl into the earth, anchoring you. Now, bring your mind to the bubbling spring point on the bottom of your feet, and open to feel the pulse of the Earth from this point. Soften, relax your body, allow yourself to release so that you can receive.

Imagine all that no longer serves you, energy that doesn't belong to you and things that you are ready to let go of, travelling down the back of your body to be released and composted into the Earth. Breathe, feel, notice and sense your bubbling spring opening to the Earth, allowing you to receive nourishment, strength and support. Stay here for as long as needed before you pick up your drum to play. Notice the support you feel after this exercise. It's easier for us to receive when we have had the opportunity to release some of the extra burdens we carry and when we feel held and secure.

Try this also before a reiki treatment and notice how it affects your practice. And it can be a useful exercise to talk clients through if they are suffering from extreme tension, anxiety and stress. We can also connect to the bubbling spring lying down with legs bent, or seated, as long as the soles of the feet are flat on the floor and spine straight. See "Release and Restore with Earth Energy" in Chapter 5, page 117.

TAKE ACTION   Meet the Spirit of Your Drum

Your drum will have a certain special quality to bring to your reiki practice and the more you play it, the more you will discover about its unique energy. When you first lay your hands on your drum, it may take you some time to get to know each other. It's up to you to find a special way to honour this connection and create the relationship. You may find that your drum has a name, or that there is a specific way that feels right to you to adorn the drum or connect to it, or even store it. There may be a specific ritual that you feel guided to do in a sacred place to help you connect. Maybe the drum needs to be left out under the full moon or in the shade of an oak tree? Keep listening and be open to what you feel guided to do.

Invite reiki to flow from your sacred space with your guides and helpers and pick up your drum. Hold in your heart the intention to connect with the spirit of your drum. Even if you have already done this, it's worth repeating!

When you feel ready, place your intention into your drum by holding it in your hands and sending reiki into the drum head. Begin to drum when you feel ready. Open yourself to connecting with the rhythm and spirit of your drum.

Let your drum know what your intention is and what you would like it to assist you with. Ask it what its power is and how it can help you in your practice.

Be open to receiving images, information, thoughts, feelings, ideas, memories, songs, names, and so on.

You may be guided, if not now but at some stage as you play your drum, to decorate it in some way. Some of my clients have painted symbols on their drum heads, or pictures of power animals or plants. Others have attached ribbons, crystals or bells.

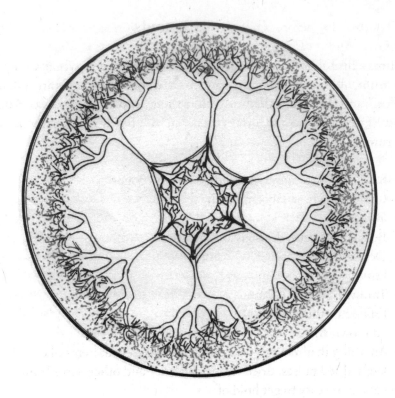

Drum heads can be decorated with spirit allies,
power animals, or aspects of nature.

The drum that was presented to me during my reiki drum training was a synthetic Remo buffalo drum. After my attunement and training I had a sense of what the drum was asking for in terms of adornment, but I'm ashamed to say that it took me many years to get round to it. I couldn't seem to find the right way to put into practice the vision that I was shown. One of the benefits of synthetic drums is that they can be easily painted with acrylic paints; however, I knew that this was not what my drum was calling for. Instead, hanging off coloured ribbons at the back of my drum, I now have four wooden hearts, each painted gold and carrying a reiki symbol. These hearts make their own sound as the drum is carried and played, and it also makes this drum unique to me.

Other Instruments

You may find that once you get started with working with sound and the drum, all sorts of other instruments and sound makers start "talking to you" and you feel called to gather them into your practice. Allow yourself to be guided and always try before you buy if you can. Common instruments used in practice are:

- Steel drums, tongue drums, djembes and gongs
- Crystal bowls or Tibetan bowls
- Flutes
- Bells, koshi bells, ocarinas and whistles
- Ocean drums
- Rattles and clappers
- Tuning forks and chimes
- Kalimbas (thumb piano)
- Your own voice
- Anything that makes a sound that appeals to you; items like seeds, dried pulses, dried leaves, seashells, and other items from nature, are easy to get hold of.

With all new tools, spend time getting to know them and sensing their energy. As with the previous exercise, let them know your intention and ask them what their power is and how they can help you in your practice. You may find that you use specific drums, rattles, bells or other instruments for specific client symptoms or particular healing patterns and techniques. Allow yourself to be guided. Don't rush out to buy; tune in and feel for what is needed in your practice. Invite in tools and instruments, play with the universe and watch how it delivers to you exactly what you need.

TAKE ACTION Make Your Own Instrument

You can make your own tools with a little creativity and imagination: by putting dry beans in a jar, you have an instant rattle. Clap your hands, hum or click your fingers – this turns you into a powerful instrument that can call to the spirit world and shift energy. There is no need to buy lots of shiny new spiritual tools or instruments; see what comes to you and if you need something then call it forward. Keep an eye out for drum- or rattle-making courses. There is great power in creating your own instruments that are unique to you, rather than buying generic items.

Healing Voices

One of the most powerful and certainly most innate instruments of sound healing is your own voice. Think about those times that you stub your toe and shout "OUCH!" out loud, or the way you might soften your voice to speak to a friend who is upset and needs comforting. Even the way you speak to clients might be different from the voice you use at home. It's unfortunate that many of us think that we can't sing and are therefore hesitant to use our voices in a treatment space; this is a waste of such a powerful instrument.

I have found making sound during reiki treatments to be a natural progression from practising reiki with the drum. I started with sounds that were more closed and one-syllable, like "ohm, hum, ooo, nee, aah, shoo, hey"; and then I gradually became more confident in stringing sounds together. I certainly don't sing a song or attempt to, or even think about what sounds I am making, but often clients comment on how beautiful the sound was that accompanied the drum. It's worth a try.

TAKE ACTION Freeing Your Voice

As you drum, relax and allow your voice to create sounds. Express yourself softly at first if that feels right, and then more openly as you start to feel more confident. Start with just you and your drum and build up, expanding your sound-making until you feel confident enough to bring the sound of your voice into your healing space or drum circles.

Reiki *Kotodama*

While we are on the subject of sound and voice, it feels essential to mention the *kotodama* of reiki. Whereas in the West we learn symbols at reiki Levels 2 and 3, each with their own unique *jumon* or mantra, Mikao Usui traditionally taught *kotodama*. These are sacred sounds that are chanted in a specific way to bridge the body and mind. The word *kotodama* means "word spirit" or "soul" and refers to the power of words or sound to make things happen.

Kotodama are sung from deep within with your whole body; the sound needs to come from your lower abdomen. In Japanese this area is called the *hara*, but you may also know it as the *dantien*. It is the physical centre of the body and balance as well as the centre of your spiritual energy. Chanting from this place of power makes the sound resonate through your whole being. One *kotodama* is chanted at a time and repeated over and over again.

This helps to bridge the body and mind. The aim of chanting *kotodama* is to realize our interconnectedness with the universe.

Each sound within the *kotodama* carries a specific meaning and forms a pattern that creates a state of being within the mind and body. There are *kotodama* for each of the reiki symbols: focus, harmony, connection and empowerment. Rather than write them down here, where you may have difficulty pronouncing them correctly and feeling their resonance, I suggest you seek further teachings. It's more beneficial to be able to hear them and speak them than to read them!

If you are already familiar with *kotodama* then consider how you could work them into your drum practice. How about using the drum as a slow, steady background beat to support your chanting?

Drums Don't Like Being Left Behind

Three years of my shamanic training were spent in sacred space over long weekends up on the Falkland Estate in Fife, Scotland. These involved staying over for a few nights in nearby accommodation. On our very first evening we were invited to leave any items behind that we would not need overnight, such as yoga mats, blankets, and so on. I grabbed my bag with my journal in and left everything else – including, foolishly, my drum. My head thought, it will be fine, I won't need it tonight and it's a little bulky to take. Everything was OK until I drove the car off the estate and turned in to the road to my accommodation.

That was when the symphony began; my drum beat a solid, deafening beat. It was as if the drum was screaming at me. Oh shit! I gulped. This drum is not happy! I knew I couldn't turn back because the space was closed down for the night. I had no choice but to continue on to my accommodation. I spoke silently to my drum, asking forgiveness, assuring her that I was coming back and apologizing like a madwoman. What a rookie mistake to make, thinking that the drum would be OK to be left in a strange place. I realized I hadn't even asked if she minded being left. I think that is why the drum felt so mad. It was as if I had disrespected her in some way. Of course we made up;

we're still creating magic together and I totally learned my lesson. Always include the drum. Don't make decisions for the drum. Ask it. Ask your guides. Ask your tools. Don't think with reason and logic where spiritual tools are concerned.

Ways to Use Reiki and the Drum

There are many ways to work with reiki and sound instruments like the drum, but the most simple way is to ask for reiki to flow through you for the highest good before you pick up the instrument. You can charge your drum with reiki by placing it between your hands for a few minutes and sending reiki, or rubbing the flat palm of your dominant hand over the drum head in a circular motion. If you are trained to reiki Level 2 or above you may like to scribe the symbols on the drum head, on your palms or in the air to assist you. When you play the drum, simply allow yourself to be guided by the sound and by the flow of reiki.

The drum and reiki can be used for techniques such as:

- Space clearing and energizing (with the power symbol *Cho Ku Rei* or *CKR*).
- Shamanic reiki journeys (travelling into the spirit world to seek guidance and/or healing for your own or your clients' issues such as power and soul retrieval).
- Reiki drum healing technique (drumming with reiki over a client as part of a reiki treatment) to help shift stagnant energies, create change and promote relaxation.
- Distance healing treatment (drumming with reiki for yourself or a client, for future events or to heal past experiences).
- Reiki drum mindset reprogramming (a reiki drum technique to help shift mindset, break a habit or manifest a new story).
- Nature connection and healing (drumming with reiki to align with the heartbeat of the Earth or to connect to the spirits of the land, nature beings or plant spirits in nature).
- Merging with reiki to receive healing, increase your ability to channel reiki, strengthen your connection and discover more about reiki energy.
- Group drumming circles or ceremony to honour specific seasons or elements or to bring extra power to group healing.

- Drumming to bring momentum to personal goals and dreams.
- Self-healing, relaxation and meditation as part of your reiki practice.

Reiki Level 2 Symbols and Your Drum

If you invite reiki to flow before you drum or listen to a drumming track, then you will be supported by the strong, nurturing and protective light of reiki during the process. Those trained in reiki Level 2 or above will be able to connect with the reiki symbols that you are guided to. Reiki Level 2 introduces you to certain symbols that represent aspects of reiki energy. Using the symbols learned at reiki Level 2 and above with the drum enhances and gives focus to the healing rhythm that flows. These symbols are widely documented in reiki books and websites and, if you have been trained to reiki Level 2, you will have been taught and attuned to the symbols shown to you by your teacher. If you are not familiar with the symbols you can still play the drum but if you do already work with them, then I urge you to introduce them into your drum practice.

Working with the drum really helps to feel the power of these symbols in another dimension. It reminds us that the symbols are not flat drawings in fancy patterns, they are aspects of reiki energy that bring specific qualities to our reiki treatments and our drumming. They are vibrations at a specific frequency, which we can experience when we drum and also when we chant their mantra. Since I started drumming the symbols, I have a whole new perspective on what they represent and I can feel them more easily.

The Level 2 symbols I am referring to are as follows:

The Power Symbol (Cho Ku Rei)

For protection, cleansing, focus and power. This symbol may be used by itself or to bring power to the other symbols. *Cho Ku Rei* is a potent and highly charged frequency. As you may have been taught in reiki Level 2, it can be used alongside the other symbols to bring power and focus the healing energies on the subject of your intention. For this reason it is possibly the most widely used symbol. It is fortunate that it is easy to remember. The power symbol can also be used by itself, for example in space clearing, protection or grounding. I like to work with the power symbol as a cloak of protection during my shamanic reiki journeys and my healing work. The *Cho Ku Rei* cloak of protection involves you calling forward the energy of the symbol and pulling it around your physical form like an energetic cloak. If at any time I feel challenged during a journey, I will call forward the power symbol and place it in between myself and the situation/form that is challenging me, or I will wrap it around me to help me feel safe. We can also do this within a reiki ball of energy or light.

The Harmony Symbol (Sei Hei Ki *or* SHK)

For promoting balance, peace and harmony. This symbol assists with emotional and mindset issues. Often used in combination with the other two symbols or with *Cho Ku Rei*. When I connect with this symbol I always do so together with the power symbol. I call on *Sei Hei Ki* whenever there is a need for harmony, peace and balance within a client or a situation. If there is a strong emotional element to the healing session or journey then I will always include this symbol. Examples of this are when a client is stressed, anxious, grieving, has experienced loss or disappointment, has relationship issues, is lacking self-love or self-respect, has recently become a parent, feels unsettled or like they don't belong. I will also use this symbol when I am helping a client create a new story, shift their mindset and adopt more positive behaviour. As part of my personal healing journey, I always call on this symbol to invite in compassion, help me soften, be less judgemental or critical of others and myself, surrender to what is and open to the love and assistance of the universe.

The Distance or Connection Symbol (Hon Sha Zey Sho Nen *or* HSZSN)

Bridges time and space, helps us to connect over a distance. Used for distance healing and to connect with the root cause of disease. This symbol is very useful to help us in travelling with our shamanic reiki journeys and meeting spirit guides in other realms. It is often used with the other symbols or with *Cho Ku Rei*. I connect with this symbol together with the power symbol, to help me make a connection. Examples of this are to help me travel to/from the shamanic worlds as part of a journey and to help me connect with a guide, a place in nature or a client. I will also work with this symbol to help me connect with the source of illness or disruptive behaviour or a specific event in the past or one that I would like to manifest in the future. I will also use this symbol, together with the others, when I am offering distance healing.

Of course if you are also attuned at reiki Master Level, you will be able to experiment with the Usui Master symbol and any others that you have been shown.

TAKE ACTION Drumming the Reiki Symbols

This is an exercise to help you sense the frequency of each symbol through the beat of your drum. For each symbol:

1. Draw and visualize the symbol on your drum. I do this with my beater or my palm.
   - You may also like to draw and visualize the symbol on your palms.
   - Repeat the symbol mantra three times to invoke its frequency. You can also chant the corresponding reiki *kotodama* as you drum if you are familiar with these. Hold in your heart the intention to call forward the energy of this symbol and be shown its power.
   - Drum when you feel ready, for 5–10 minutes.
   - You may feel yourself merging with the symbol. Note down how you feel and how you felt while you were drumming this symbol.
   - Notice what the energy of the space you are in feels like.
2. Repeat this for each symbol.
3. Then practise working with all of the symbols together. Charge your drum with all of them (by drawing and visualizing them onto your drum head). Drum each of the symbols in turn and allow the drum to guide you. Notice how this feels and how it informs your practice.

Throughout the exercises in this book you will come across the phrases "connect to the symbols" and "charge the drum with the symbols". What this refers to is your own unique way of inviting the energy of these aspects of reiki into your treatment space. You may find that one or a combination of the following methods are ways that appeal, or you may be guided to create your own symbol invocation ritual.

- Visualize the symbols and embody their energy.
- Draw them in the air with your hand or drum beater.
- Draw them on your palms and place your palms onto the drum head, holding or rubbing the drum with the flat of your hand.
- Draw them onto the drum head with your drum beater.
- Chant the individual *kotodama*.
- Drum the energy and frequency of the symbols.

Charging the drum with reiki.

TAKE A BEAT

This chapter threw you in at the deep end with the mechanics of sound and what a powerful healer the drum can be, as well as offering you a glimpse of the historic role this ancient practice has played throughout the world. You will also have a clearer picture now of what to consider before you get your own instrument and how it can be played with the addition of reiki symbols. Developing your relationship with your drum and any other healing tools that you use, together with your relationship with your guides, is key to the efficacy of your personal growth and healing work. The following chapters are going to show you step by step how to do just that.

3

Journeying with the Drum

The shamanic journey is a simple and traditional technique that allows us to step into a place of expanded consciousness with the repetitive beat of a drum, rattle, dance, chanting, psychoactive plants or a combination of some of these. Leaving ordinary reality behind in this way is necessary for the shamanic practitioner to access the spirit worlds, meet their guides and obtain healing or information.

Altered states of consciousness are in fact very common. You may have found yourself in an altered state after a deep session of reiki. You might have found it difficult to come back to reality after a session, as if part of you has been elsewhere. When I am giving a client a treatment I often feel like I have gone somewhere else, like I am no longer a human in the room but have tapped into and am connected with something so much greater than me. I also feel this during my qigong practice and when it comes to completion I feel surprised at how small my physical body is compared to all that I can energetically sense when I am in the energy field.

During a reiki session I often feel the presence of spirit guides and helpers, either my own or those connected to the client, and my intuition is heightened. I am also shown many things with my inner vision and other inner senses. I feel that the practice of reiki helps us to connect to this trance state quite easily. And it is even easier with the use of the drum. The drum facilitates the shift that is needed in our brainwaves to move out of the beta state in which we normally operate.

You can practise the journey technique by listening to a drumming track or having a friend drum for you; but you will find that it's quite a different experience when you are able to drum for yourself. Reiki combines very well with shamanic journeys – you simply ask reiki to flow, to be with you for the duration; and you can invoke the distance/ connection symbol as you begin, to help you access the other worlds. Other symbols and drumming rhythms can be used throughout the journey to guide you, as I will explain.

What Is Journeying Like?

This is rather like trying to describe how a client will experience reiki. A journey experience is unique to you and will be different each time. It can be like a lucid dream in which you are able to influence the dreamscape around you. It might be very vivid, or colourful; you might find yourself in all sorts of odd situations – you might fly or swim, or do many things that in your ordinary reality aren't possible, like travel to places in the blink of an eye, ride on the back of an eagle, breathe underwater, chat to spirits of ancestors who departed the Earth long ago. This is where a shamanic journey differs from meditation; in shamanic journeying you have to take action, ask questions, go and look for things, whereas in meditation you usually remain passive, just noticing what is happening in the inner landscape in which you are immersed.

Why Is the Journey Important?

The journey is a valuable technique for your own personal development and well-being, which is why I wanted to discuss it early in the book. It can reconnect you to your power, restore a sense of wholeness, help you meet guides and develop and trust your inner knowing and compass. For me, discovering that there is another reality out there, other than the one I am living, brought a huge sense of relief and helped open my eyes to new possibilities. It has helped me curiously question my beliefs and ways of thinking and behaving (and those of others) with a new level of compassion and acceptance.

In the journey you ride the drumbeat (with reiki supporting you) and merge with the creative vibration of the unified field. Here, as part of the unified field or web of life that connects us all, you can drop your current pattern or life story and open to a new wave of potential that is your true nature. In this way the drum frees you from your current story and helps you attune to your intuitive frequency.

Though the journey process can feel strange at first, as with reiki it's a case of practice, and learning through your direct experience. Once you feel confident with the process, then you can drum for others and help them discover the magic of the journey state. Throughout these pages you will sometimes find me referring to the shamanic journey as the shamanic reiki journey; the difference is the addition of reiki to support and guide you. As a reiki practitioner, after your attunement reiki is always with you; this is why when we journey, we don't journey without it, we invite it to flow with us. I will be sharing various ways that we can make the most of reiki throughout our journeys.

There is no script for a shamanic journey, you simply allow it to unfold and just partake willingly with your intention in your heart. However, there are a few guidelines and common pitfalls that trip people up, so I wanted to offer you a roadmap to assist you with your adventures.

Three Worlds: Accessed from the World Tree

Traditionally the other worlds are mapped into three worlds, the Upper World, Middle World and Lower World, which I explain below. This model is consistent throughout many indigenous cultures and acts as a useful map that helps us to navigate the shamanic worlds. With your intention you can explore the different worlds. Each has a different quality, so you will find yourself drawn to different worlds depending on the nature of your journey.

Three Worlds	Qualities
Upper World	A light and airy world accessed by travelling upwards. This could be done, for example, by climbing the branches of a tree, a mountain or a ladder, flying on a carpet, or getting into an elevator. In this world you may encounter light beings, angels, stars, ascended Masters, or planets. This is the realm of unmanifest potential and higher knowledge. If you wanted to ask a question about reiki, or meet Dr Usui, then you would journey up here.
Middle World	The spiritual aspect of this earthly reality, where you can meet nature spirits, spirits of land and places. I access this by imagining I am walking outside of my front door. It is here that I spend a lot of time connecting to the plant spirits of my garden in my practice of plant spirit reiki.
Lower World	A rich and sensuous world accessed by travelling downwards, often through the roots of a tree or a crack in the earth, or swimming down to the bottom of the sea. Here you will meet ancestors, power animals, crystals and the past.

While these worlds are fascinating to explore, each offering different qualities for our healing and guidance, I find that beginners can often get overly worried about which world they "should be" travelling to. At first make it part of your intention to explore each of them and then, as you feel more confident and develop a deeper relationship with your guides, allow them to guide you.

Accessing the Shamanic Worlds

The shamanic worlds are accessed through an entry point in this reality. Traditionally the mythical world tree acts as this portal; you can travel down its roots into the lower world, climb its trunk into the upper world or stay with it to experience the middle world. This is certainly a very useful starting point and you can use this concept if it feels aligned with your beliefs. You may know a tree in this reality that you can imagine yourself walking to that could be your access point.

Alternatively, you may know of a cave, a stone circle, a lake, a bridge or other places that carry meaning for you and are easy to sense and which will act as your entryway. As you connect with them in your journey state, they may look different and may even appear as doorways. Over time this will shift. You may also find that connecting with and visualizing the distance/connection symbol is your portal.

My journeying practice has changed a lot since my early days. I am now much more trusting of my spirit team to simply take me to where I need to go and show me what it is that is needed. I breathe into my heart and allow my heart to expand with the beat of the drum to open this doorway within. However, the general characteristics of the process remain the same. I most often access the upper worlds on the back of an eagle or by climbing a tree. If a doorway appears in the trunk of a tree, then I find myself walking down into the Earth; or I often dive into a lake and swim down to reach the lower world. Since I enjoy connecting with the spirits of the plants in my garden, I spend a lot of time in the middle world. This I access easily by seeing myself walk out of my back door and into my garden.

TAKE ACTION   Sensing Your Entry Point

Before you experiment with a full journey, it may help you to drum in your prepared space and feel, see and sense yourself at the entry point that will connect you with the shamanic worlds. Consider what places in nature you know in this reality that have meaning for you. Perhaps there is a tree in your garden that you admire, or a natural spring or cave that you have visited that feels powerful, or maybe the distance/connection symbol is calling you. Invite reiki to flow as you drum, relax and allow the beat of the drum to come naturally. Invite it in through your heart. Close your eyes and imagine yourself leaving the space that you are in and stepping outside into the world. Feel, see and sense yourself travelling to your chosen point of entry. You may wish to dive deep into your own heart. Just relax as the drumbeat guides you.

Open up all of your senses to experience this place in nature and notice as you drum what you can feel in the air around you, what you observe, together with any sounds or scents in the air. Sometimes colours may feel brighter and your senses may feel more alert. Notice how you physically feel in your body at this entry point and what emotions are surfacing for you. Allow yourself to feel the potential that lies within your portal/doorway; permit yourself to feel excited at the possibility of travelling to other worlds.

When you feel ready, feel, see and sense yourself leaving your access point and returning into your space, back to this reality.

Note down anything that feels significant about this experience and make sure you are fully grounded back in this reality before heading back to your busy life.

Why Practise the Shamanic Reiki Journey?

- To receive personal healing.
- To explore other realities and possibilities.
- To find answers and solutions to issues.
- To meet guides, helping spirits, light beings or ancestors and receive information, guidance, or healing.
- For diagnostic journeys (before a client treatment – to be discussed later).
- To help clients deeply relax, meet guides, receive specific healing like power retrieval or soul restoration and receive insight.

Shamanic Reiki Journey Preparation

As with your reiki practice, an essential part of your work for shamanic journeying lies in the preparation of yourself and your space. Making sure that you allow enough time for sufficient preparation can help you get the most out of your drumming journeys. It's much easier to connect with the other realms if you are not rushing but are in a calm and relaxed state, in a clear space with a clear intention.

- Prepare yourself and your space.
- Invite in your helpers.
- Ask reiki to flow.
- Use an affirmation to assist you.
- Consider your intention and motivation.

Sacred Container – Preparation of Self

There are many reiki techniques, meditations and activities such as yoga and qigong that can centre you so that you are ready to give a treatment or journey with your drum. You can even simply focus on your breath. If you have been practising reiki for a while I'm sure that you will already have your go-to methods and rituals. Feeling safe and protected from the influence of negative energies or energies that do not belong to you is also important. In order to set up a protective boundary when you are doing a healing, a simple technique is to visualize white, purple or gold light surrounding you and spreading out from you.

Reiki Techniques for Cleansing Your Energy Field

You may already be familiar with reiki techniques such as the reiki shower technique and *Hatsurei Ho*, which function to clear the aura of negative energies and cleanse us from the inside out with the breath. These practices can also help to strengthen your connection to reiki and become a stronger conduit for the energy.

Strengthening your light is another reiki technique available to you. There are several variations, depending on your knowledge of the reiki symbols, but each has the same intention: to strengthen your personal energy and light that surrounds you.

The simplest version uses the power symbol; other versions may include the Master symbols. Draw or visualize a large power symbol in front of you and step into it or pull it around you like a cloak. Then draw or visualize the symbol in each of your energy centres from your root up to your crown with the intention that each of them is clear, aligned with your true frequency, open and flowing with reiki. You are surrounding yourself with the light of reiki and lower frequencies will be transmuted by this light, thus protecting you.

Of course, if you prefer to keep things simple then invite reiki to flow with the intention that it cleanses your energy field and releases stagnant energy. You can meditate in *gassho* or place your hands over your body to focus on certain areas where you sense stagnation or blockages.

Inviting In Your Helpers

If you have a guide who you feel is especially protective, you may like to invite them to be with you also. For example, one of my guides has a shield and I invite him to be by my side for client treatments or as I journey. I also have another guide who is a tree, and to ask for extra protection I sense myself stepping into the trunk of the tree and becoming the tree. Or you may feel aligned to angelic beings such as Archangel Michael. Having a guide who you feel aligned with as a protecting force can feel very supportive. For this very reason I recommended journeying with your drum to connect with a guide, if you do not have one already. I will walk you through this exercise later.

Crystals and Talismans

I like to work with labradorite, amethyst, rose or clear quartz crystals but I also have a fondness for any rock or stone that feels powerful for me. Select crystals or simple pebbles that you feel drawn to work with for protection. Many people also like to have an amulet to wear for this purpose.

Sacred Container: Space Clearing and Creating Sacred Space

There are two parts to creating your sacred container. It's advised to firstly cleanse the space, and follow this by using rituals, invocations or reiki to create sacred space that is filled with light and high frequency. Spaces, like people, can retain energy from previous participants or situations; as part of your reiki practice you will already be aware of the importance of cleansing the area of any stagnant or negative energy and filling it with positive energy. Candles, incense, essential oils, room sprays and the power symbol are all common tools, but a simple clap of the hands and burst of fresh air can also be effective – and there is nothing like beating your drum!

Shamanic practitioners often create sacred space by calling in the sacred directions of the medicine wheel with prayer, drumbeats or a rattle. The points on the medicine wheel align with the directions of a compass and their corresponding elements in nature, colours, seasons of the year, stages of life, animals and plants. The medicine wheel is a concept used by many traditions worldwide to help us navigate the energy flow of the seasons, cycles of the year and stages of our lives, and therefore it has many interpretations. I work with a variation of the Celtic wheel of the year because that resonates with me, but if you are more drawn to learn from the Native American medicine wheels then look there for inspiration instead. It is a rich and powerful concept that will help you really tune in to the wisdom and the power of nature. The directions – East, South, West, and North – are typically represented by a corresponding colour, such as black, red, yellow and white. The directions can represent:

- Stages of life: birth, youth, adult (or elder), death.
- Seasons of the year: spring, summer, winter, autumn.
- Aspects of life: spiritual, emotional, intellectual, physical.
- Elements of nature: fire (or sun), air, water, earth.
- Animals: eagle, bear, wolf, buffalo and many others.
- Ceremonial plants: tobacco, sweetgrass, sage, cedar.
- Phases of the moon: waxing, full, waning, new moon.

The elements and energies of the medicine wheel can be physically represented in your sacred space or on your altar to bring in their qualities. The following are some ideas and their corresponding directions. Note that this is different in different traditions; they will have more meaning for you if you connect with each of them and discover them for yourself. Choose what feels right for you.

Elements	Corresponding Directions
Air (in the east)	May be represented by words that are spoken or written; prayers; songs; leaves or spring flowers; feathers, butterflies or incense.
Fire (in the south)	Often represented by a candle, a sunflower, movement, passion, fiery colours like red and orange or something creative such as a work of art.
Water (in the west)	Water can be placed in a cup or represented by a lily, quartz crystal, a shell, images of the moon, the ocean or a river.
Earth (in the north)	Earth can be represented with a bowl of soil, crystals or stones. You can also use food such as bread, chocolate or nuts.
Centre	This is you!

In my previous book *Plant Spirit Reiki* I discussed in detail some of the plants that I like to bring in to create sacred space. Whenever you make use of plant materials, remember to say a prayer to invite the spirit of the plant into your space for extra potency.

Some of my favourite ways to create sacred space are:

- Create an altar or centrepiece with natural objects like flowers, stones and feathers.
- Light a candle.
- Invite reiki to flow.
- Burn herbs or diffuse essential oils such as:
    - Garden sage: to purify people and places.
    - Mugwort: to help with vision.
    - Rosemary: to call to helping spirits for protection, to help focus and promote clarity.
    - Lavender: to bring in positive energies to a space after cleansing and invoke a calming atmosphere.
    - Frankincense, cedarwood or myrrh: to assist with protection and meditation.
    - Clary sage: for inner connection to the dreamtime.
    - Rose: for opening the heart (receiving/giving).

- Add flower essences such as walnut or yarrow to a spray bottle and spritz in the air for protection.
- Drum and rattle.
- Call in your helping spirits and guides.

If you are clearing the space for others, don't assume they will be OK with fragrances, essential oils and burning herbs. Always check for allergies and sensitivities – these are more common than we think!

Creating Sacred Space with Reiki

After you have cleared your space you may wish to invite in reiki to flow, as well as guides, angels, spirit helpers, ancestors and compassionate beings, to assist you with your work. It can be as simple as asking them to come, reciting a sacred prayer or rattling for them as a signal. You can also use the reiki symbols such as the power symbol or the Tibetan Master symbol to clear away stagnant energies from a space by placing them in the corners of the room or at the centre.

Another simple way is to simply sit in *gassho* and visualize reiki flowing through you out into the room. You may visualize whatever colour light reiki represents to you, such as rainbow light, golden light, white or diamond light. The colour may even change depending on the quality of the energy that is being called forward. You may also decide to visualize other reiki symbols such as the harmony symbol to bring its peaceful qualities into your space.

To keep your space clear you can also set a powerful intention that nothing intrude on your sacred space.

TAKE ACTION Space Clearing with the Drum

Invite reiki to flow in the way that you have been taught. For me, I simply place my hands into *gassho* (prayer position) and close my eyes and invite reiki to flow for my highest good and the highest good of all beings.

Set your intention to clear the energy or clear the space of stagnant or negative energies for the highest good and bring forward positive energy of reiki. You can speak this out loud or you can simply hold it in your heart.

Pick up your drum and hold it in your hands. If you are attuned to reiki Level 2 I recommend visualizing or drawing the power symbol onto your drum head, or you could simply draw the power symbol onto your dominant hand and place that on the drum. If you are reiki Level 1 then simply hold the drum in your hands with your intention to clear the space.

Start drumming when you feel ready. You can intentionally drum the power symbol out into the room, or simply send reiki with the drum. Drum for as long as you feel is needed; you might want to drum into the corners of the room, drum to the sky, drum to the Earth, drum to the four directions. You might feel yourself called to flow in different directions in different areas of the space depending on how you feel guided.

Remember your intention is to clear the space and shift the energy. I also recommend opening windows to allow the energy to clear.

You might also wish to use your voice or other instruments or even play music.

Develop your own drumming ritual to clear and open your sacred space.

Affirmations for Your Journey

When you start to journey with your drum you might harbour a niggling doubt that insists that you won't be able to do it, so as you start out it can be useful to create a positive affirmation to assist you. Affirmations are a valuable way of helping our subconscious mind accept beliefs, behaviours and actions. Using simple affirmations before a journey will help you release any fears or anxiety you may have about the journey and accept the experience with non-judgement. Examples of useful affirmations are as follows; make use of those that feel helpful and relevant to you.

"I am more than my physical body."

"I am capable of experiencing expanded states of consciousness and journeying into other realms and realities."

"I release any and all fears and I know that I am safe and protected."

"I release any and all judgement and expectation about my experience."

"I know and trust that my heart and mind will remember my journey and the teachings that are important."

"I've got this and the universe has got me."

TAKE ACTION Create Your Affirmation

For your drumming journeys, create an affirmation in your own words that helps you to feel at ease and shift any doubt or fear you may be carrying. Write it down.

Intentions and Motivation

As you will have experienced in your reiki practice, intention is key to the healing process. Reiki is activated by intention. Similarly, Jonathan Goldman, a leading sound expert, has collated much research in his field, and he has found that intention is also key in sound healing.

It won't surprise you to hear, then, that one of the most important elements of any shamanic journey work is intention. Journeying with a focused and clear intention is key to success. This is the rudder that will steer you through and keep you on track. Give this some thought before you begin.

Equally important is your motivation, so tune in to what purpose your journey is serving. Is it just to benefit you? How can it benefit all beings?

It may be helpful to write it down to help it really sink in and hold it in your heart.

An example intention to start with might be:

> *My intention is to journey to meet with a guide to help me with my shamanic reiki practice and be shown what I need to know now.*

With intentions, ask to be shown rather than asking a yes or no question. This opens the doorway for spirit to send you omens and dreams, vibration and frequency.

Avoid asking "why?", too – helping spirits can be really encouraging even when there is a big challenge ahead because spirit knows that challenges help us grow!

You can always ask multiple questions as you get more experienced with the journey process, though my advice is to keep it simple as you begin. For example: "Show me where reiki is needed." "Show me the nature of this issue."

Avoid asking	Rephrase to
Why is this client always late?	Show me what I am not seeing or what needs healing with this client.
Should I work with this client?	What will I learn if I work with this client?
Is this the right job for me?	Show me what changes will occur in my life if I take this job.
How can I reach more clients with my healing work?	In what ways may more clients be reached with my healing work?

Useful Intention Formats

- Please give me help with healing ... (the issue).
- Please show me how to deal with ... (the issue).
- Please show me what help is available for ... (the issue) and how it can be manifested.
- Please give me teaching on ...
- Please help me transform ...
- Please show me what is needed for ...
- Please help me meet a guide to help me learn about ...
- Please show me how to develop/nourish/grow stronger ...

When I first started to journey, I found the experience so incredible and exciting that I easily lost my focus and allowed myself to get sidetracked. I would forget the reason I was journeying and what question I had wanted to ask. While this was interesting and fun as fuel for my curiosity and imagination, it meant that often I was frustrated after a journey because when I looked at my intention, I realized that it hadn't been met so the purpose to my actions were lost. If you often get distracted then write your intention down to get it clear in your mind, and keep it simple so that you can remember it and stay focused on your direction.

Shamanic Journeying with Reiki and the Drum – Technique

A classic shamanic journey taught in Western shamanic practice has a very clear structure that helps us to access and sustain an altered state of consciousness, and this is very useful as a map to guide you when you are getting started. The process is characterized by rapid beats at the start of the journey (around 220 beats per minute – yes, that is fast) in order to help you travel into the other realms; the beat will then change, signalling that you are in the journey and it's time to meet your guides and ask your questions. After a while the beat changes again, which signals that it's almost time to come back to your reality. This gives you an opportunity to say thank you and reverse your footsteps in the journey (which also helps you to feel more grounded when you return and to remember what happened). You will then hear a call-back beat, which is the same rapid beat that you heard at the start of the journey, calling you back to your reality.

It can feel like there is a lot to remember, but don't let yourself worry about what you "should" be doing or how you think you "should" be drumming; it's more important to relax and allow the drum to take you on a journey. It's often easier for beginners to start with longer journeys of about twenty minutes or more in order to fully relax and allow the drum to shift your brainwaves into the altered state. There isn't a wrong way to journey or to drum. If you struggle with being too much in your head with anxious thoughts, then spend 15 minutes prior to the journey giving yourself a self-reiki treatment to help calm you and relax your mind.

If you are a trained reiki Level 2 practitioner or above then you can work with the symbols during your journey process. The distance/connection symbol can help you as you travel back and forwards from the shamanic worlds, and the other symbols may feel useful to connect with during your journey to bring extra power, protection or connection with guides or to show your gratitude at the end of your experience.

Below is an example of how you can work with the different symbols and change of drumbeat to guide yourself or a client through a journey.

As you become more familiar with your drum and the journey technique, you will simply follow your intuition and allow the drum to guide you. You may like to record yourself drumming so that you can practise this shamanic reiki journey technique. Most phones have a voice recorder app that can be used for this, or alternatively there is Audacity free audio software, which can be used on a laptop.

- Prepare yourself and your space so that you are relaxed and feel at ease.
- Create a positive affirmation if you carry fear or doubt.

- Focus on your clear intention.
- Ask reiki to flow in the way that you have been taught and pick up your drum (place the symbols into the drum if you know them, by holding the drum in your hands).
- Visualize or feel yourself wrapped inside a ball of reiki light and energy to keep you safe.
- Enter the journey by connecting with your access point (tree or place in nature).
- Drum rapidly with the distance/connection symbol to help you. Feel yourself crossing through the portal and travelling into another world.
- Change the beat.
- Now you are in the journey, spend as long as you need exploring. Feel the beat of the drum here and allow yourself to be guided.
- You may feel guided to use the symbols *CKR* and *SHK* here also.
- You may also feel guided to give reiki to situations, beings, images, and so on that appear in the journey.
- After about fifteen minutes, change the beat (this may occur naturally).
- Wrap up the journey for a couple of minutes, then offer your thanks.
- When you feel ready to come back, change the beat.
- Drum quickly with the distance/connection symbol to return to this reality.
- Give 9–12 slow beats to indicate finish.
- Express your gratitude.
- Play a piece of music and integrate the session with ten minutes of self-reiki or client reiki.
- Ground, disconnect and close down your space.

Grounding

As part of your reiki practice you will already have your own methods for grounding after connecting with reiki. After being in the journey state it is important to make sure both you and any others involved are grounded and connected to the Earth.

There are many different techniques; you may like to experiment with the following:

1. Bring your attention to your feet and imagine roots growing out of them, reaching deep down and holding you to the Earth. Even better – go outside and walk barefoot on the grass!
2. Simply stamp your feet and clap your hands.
3. Use crystals such as hematite – an excellent healing and grounding stone.
4. Have a cup of tea and a snack.
5. Take some fresh air or breathe deeply into your belly.
6. Use the reiki power symbol, *Cho Ku Rei*. Drawn or drummed at the feet it is a useful and easy tool to work with.

Integration

After a journey or altered state it's imperative that you allow the process to settle so that your body, mind and spirit can integrate all of the experience. For me the magic often comes in those precious moments that follow a journey. After the loud excitement and flurry of activity that the drum brings, as I pause in quiet and allow the pieces of myself to slot back together, often snippets of gold – guidance, wisdom and insight – are revealed to me. I recommend having a piece of music to play after you have finished your drumming so that you can rest for the duration of the piece and allow the integration of your full experience to take place. This will not only help you remain open to guidance that is available for you but will also allow you time to ground and fully return to this reality. One of the tracks that I am known for playing is "Returning" by Jennifer Berezan. Don't be tempted to rush the integration after a journey or drumming of any kind. It is a valuable part of your experience. The drum is a powerful tool that physically shifts energy within and around you, so you may be physically different following a drumming session. Pause, ground and allow your altered state to come back together again into the new way that it wants to be after the session.

Close Down Your Space

Be really clear that your connection with the spirit world and your journey is complete. You will already have your own established rituals for doing this as part of your reiki practice. You may like to use the reiki symbols, say a closing prayer, thank your guides or burn herbs or incense to clear the space.

Note-Taking and Journaling

At first your journeys might be unclear or confusing, perhaps a wild ride with lots of happening or maybe a darkness in which nothing seems to show itself to you or nothing much seems to take place. Whatever your experience, write down what feels most significant about what you sense and feel. Your notes will turn into precious breadcrumbs to guide your path ahead as you look back over what you have written. I have reams and reams of dog-eared journals, battered notebooks, and some random bits of paper with scrawls in pen and coloured pencils, all carrying messages of magic from my meditations, dreams, self-reiki sessions, plant spirit reiki encounters and drumming journeys. Every so often I pick one off the shelf and open a page at random to read an insight from years ago. The messages are always powerful and still relevant.

Keeping records of each time you receive information from guides or those in the other realms is an essential part of developing your understanding. Each experience holds a key piece of information that has been shown to you to help you. Even though many of our encounters or experiences don't seem to make sense to our logical mind, please don't neglect to write them down. Everything in a journey is part of the guidance and healing and the answer to your question! Always note down even the smallest of details as they might carry huge significance. Most of us think that we will remember such a bright or vibrant idea, but sadly that's often not the case; these snippets might as well be written on disappearing ink. Journals are valuable; they are YOUR personal oracle. At first you might not be able to note down every snippet and may only manage to summarize your experience with just one word or a doodle; however, it can be useful to note the following information:

- Date
- Your intention
- Your journey method: e.g., drumming for yourself, listening to a track, self-reiki meditation
- Which guides you connected with
- Key points of the experience that feel significant
- Key message/guidance provided
- How you felt afterwards
- What has shifted (can be added weeks or even years later).

Looking back over old journals can highlight patterns and provide insight into current issues. It's also often a gentle nudge to integrate guidance that you've been given but might have failed to acknowledge or take action on.

I find my journals give me hope. Sometimes I read through sections and they appear so magical that I don't believe I could have written them or remember that I did! The spirit world doesn't operate in the linear time model that the human world has adopted and adheres to so stubbornly. You may find, as you look through old journals, that the answer to the question you are looking for is on your pages.

Expressing a journey creatively can help you to find meaning.

Guides and Allies

You may already be familiar with guides and spirit helpers from your reiki practice, but, as you develop your shamanic experience, new guides will join you to enhance and bring a new element into your shamanic reiki practice. If you are not familiar with guides and spirit helpers, think about a trusted friend, a non-judgemental helper, ally or wise one who you can turn to for support, guidance and assistance with all sorts of things. As your experience of reiki grows, so too will your awareness of spiritual guides or beings of light who sometimes work with the power of reiki. These guides may come into our awareness and provide assistance when we are doing a healing or during self-practice. It is not unusual to find that after a healing your client may comment that they felt as if there was another pair of hands on them. These guides are gentle, loving and safe spirits that work only for good.

Everybody has their own personal guide. Sometimes, when we are doing a healing, these spirits may make contact with us and give us insight and healing techniques that can help our client to heal. Trust your instincts if you see or sense someone guiding you. Your own guides and your reiki guides will make sure that you are protected. If the presence feels good then I tend to go with it; if it feels intrusive or I feel unsure then I simply say no. Remember you are in charge; and it helps to set clear boundaries around who or what energies your healing space is available to.

The more you connect with your drum and reiki, the more likely you are to meet guides that can assist you in different ways. As you develop your shamanic skillset and get more familiar with the shamanic universe, different guides and spirit helpers will come forward to work with you, each offering a different perspective or focus to your healing intention.

As a healer it is important that you develop your relationship with the energies that are greater than you (the spirit that flows through all things), and the more experience you gain, the more trust you will engender from your relationship with your own spirit helpers. From this trust you will become more confident with your healing gifts and intuition.

Guides come in many forms; they may appear in human form or as colours, sounds, sensations or vibrations. Release your expectations and remain open. Your guides will appear in the way that most appeals to you, and will accompany you as you journey with your drum and work with clients. Ask them questions and get to know them.

Your guide may appear in forms such as:

- Ancestors
- Angels
- Animal guides
- Beings of light
- Birds
- Plant allies
- Stones/crystals
- Elements e.g., wind, fire, water, Mother Earth
- Nature beings
- Mythological creatures
- Light or vibration/sound
- Human form
- Wise woman or tribal elder
- Reiki Master

Guides communicate in many different ways, as you may have already experienced as part of your reiki practice. Consider how you receive information or which of your special senses feel most receptive. The list is endless, but you may receive information in some of the following ways:

- Orbs of light
- Felt sensations in your body
- Emotions
- Downloads
- Transmission of energy or healing
- Knowing
- Numbers
- Oracle cards
- Visions and dreams
- Synchronicity, omens or signs
- Shifts in energy or temperature
- Song/sound
- Smell or taste

TAKE ACTION Journey to Connect with a Guide

If you only ever do one journey – make it this one! Connecting with a guide is the start of a special relationship that, if nurtured, reaps bountiful rewards over time. When you connect with guides you are connecting to a higher part of yourself and this can be a highly emotional and joyful experience that expands your heart.

Follow the previous guidance on preparing yourself and setting up your space.

Write down your intention to "meet with a guide to show me the shamanic worlds".

You can either choose to drum for yourself or select a drumming track.

As the journey begins, imagine yourself walking out of your front door into nature. Hold the intention in your heart to meet a guide.

From your place in nature (your chosen access point), explore with all of your senses and be open to what is there. Permit yourself to feel excited and energized with the expectation of meeting a guide. Feel the potentiality of this and whatever the guide may turn out to be. Open yourself to the unlimited possibilities of what the universe can provide for you.

Notice what or who is there with you in nature. Who or what are you able to see or hear? There may be something that is appearing in the corner of your vision.

Ask whatever is there if they are a guide who will show you around. Feel for a response.

Wait patiently and feel for what comes. Keep waiting and ask again if you don't feel a response.

Keep all of your senses open and notice how you feel. You will need to learn how they communicate with you. It may help you to invoke the distance/connection reiki 2 symbol to help you make the connection.

They may not say anything at all, they may show you something, you may stay together in silence. You may not see them; you may just sense a presence.

Open up your senses to the whole experience.

Feel this resonance flow through your body.

When it is ready to come back, thank the guide (or the experience) and retrace your footsteps to return to your front door and back into the room you are in.

Allow yourself time to integrate this experience and journal on your feelings and what this experience has to teach you.

How do you feel knowing that you have a guide who will accompany you whenever you journey into other worlds or whenever you need it in this reality?

Maybe you feel disappointed because you didn't sense a presence or you didn't feel it communicated with you. Remember you can repeat this journey as many times as you wish. As you spend more time with this guide you will learn how to communicate with it and be able to ask further questions. You will also be able to ask the guide to show you the shamanic worlds and explore together.

It took years for me to acknowledge and become fully aware of one of my now most trusted guides. His presence, which I had always felt during journeys and also during reiki practice, was so familiar to me and so much a part of me that it took a long while for me to recognise this presence as a wise guide. One day the penny finally dropped and I realised that this incredible, kind guide had always been there! It felt very powerful to finally recognise and honour this wisdom as part of me. Don't be surprised if you feel a strong familiarity between yourself and your guide(s) – they are an extension of you!

If you tried this journey while drumming for yourself, maybe you can experiment again by using a drumming track. Record one for yourself on your phone or get a friend to help.

The Return of the Crow, January 2022

She was waiting, mother crow
Biding her time, waiting for the storm and the fire, the rage,
   the desire.
Ripped out of my (own) skin by the talons of the hawk,
The messenger had come.
We flew, me dangling by my shoulders
Legs flaying, swaying, shaking off the old,
Releasing all the gunk that bound me to the small box of the
   past.
Opening me to what is here for me.
When will I truly open?
When the inferno is beneath me
When the village is burning
That is the signal.
I see the firebirds, my kin, rising from the ashes.

Crescendos of rainbow colour,
Making waves and curves in the sky
Black and rainbow
My soul retrieval guide appears and so too does blackbird
They bring gifts
The drumbeat falters
My wings can no longer remain bound and contained,
My span expands
My wings unfurl, like rickety bones and rusty mechanics
They unfurl in a deep, dark intensity
All black
Raven black
Crow is back

Get to Know Your Spirit Guides

The shamanic path is often referred to as *the path of direct revelation*. When I first heard that, I hadn't got a clue what it meant. What I now understand is that it refers to the practice of shamanism as being a skill that is nurtured through direct experience and participation. In other words, start doing it and experience it for yourself!

The success, clarity and depth of understanding of your shamanic endeavours relies on your relationships with spirit helpers and guides. The more you work with them and create a relationship, the deeper your understanding will be as you learn how they communicate and how to interpret their guidance. The following pointers may be useful to remember:

- Honour your relationship with guides as they appear and develop your relationship with them.
- Be open and non-judgemental.
- Release your expectations of yourself and of your guides.
- Ask questions about who they are, what their power is and how they can help you.
- Keep asking; if something seems unclear, then journey again!

Shamanic Journeying Checklist

- Prepare your space.
- Call in your guides and helpers (and reiki!).
- Prepare yourself.
- Tune in to your intention and your motivation.
- Invite a guide to be with you.
- Drum or listen to a drumming track when you feel ready.
- Relax and release judgement and expectation.
- Allow the beat of the drum to take you on a journey.
- Use the distance symbol to help you make a connection to the other worlds.
- Keep your focus on your intention.
- Explore with curiosity and open all of your senses.
- Work with reiki symbols as you feel guided.
- Let go of control.
- Trust.
- Ask questions.
- Complete the journey and give thanks.
- Ground yourself and integrate the experience.
- Write down key points.
- Close your space when you are done.
- Make sure you act on any guidance given.

TAKE ACTION Explore the Shamanic Worlds

When you feel you have met a guide, the next step is to journey with them into the shamanic worlds.

Suggested intention: "To journey with my guide to explore the shamanic worlds and be shown what I need to know now."

As with the previous journey, connect with your guide at your entry point and, as the drumbeat speeds up to carry you across, allow yourself to travel through your portal into the shamanic worlds. This might mean you are pulled upwards or downwards, or you may find yourself walking across a bridge or flying on a bird or even taking an elevator. I find working with the distance/connection symbol is very useful at this stage.

Observe what plays out with childlike curiosity, sense with your whole being and ask questions. Work with other reiki symbols if you feel guided.

When the journey comes to an end, return the way you came and thank your guide. Play music to integrate the experience, as before, and allow yourself time to fully ground and feel present in the now. Note down anything that feels significant about this experience.

You can repeat the journey with your guide to travel to the specific worlds, to meet other guides, helping spirits, ancestors or receive information that will inform your practice and help you make positive life changes. I often find that when I reach my entry point, the drumbeat automatically pulls me forward into the shamanic worlds and once I am "on the other side" through the portal, it is here that I meet my guide. It might be the same for you. Others find that their guide is waiting for them at their entry point. You can ask your guide to be wherever you need them to be, so experiment with what you feel comfortable with. It's always advisable to move through the shamanic worlds with the help of a guide because they can show you things, support you and keep you safe.

Shamanic Reiki Drum Journeys to Explore

The journey is an experience that requires practice. Yes, practitioners can journey for you and you, when you feel confident, may journey to request information on behalf of others. However, there is nothing like creating your own connections with spirit helpers and experiencing the shamanic worlds for yourself. The more you practise, the more will be revealed to you. Journeying is like a muscle that can be trained. Practise listening to audio drumming tracks or a recording that you have made, and also practise drumming for yourself. Experiment with which journey experience you enjoy the most and find most informative.

Here are some additional ideas for journeys to start with:

- Journey to meet the spirit of your drum or other spiritual tools that you work with, like crystals or flower essences, and ask to be shown how they can help you.
- Journey to meet a guide to help you with your shamanic reiki treatments.
- Journey to meet a guide to act as a protector – an essential journey to keep you safe during your practice.
- Journey to explore the different shamanic worlds individually and be shown what you need to know now about them.
- Journey to connect with the source of reiki or the energy of the individual symbols.

- Journey to meet Usui and other ascended reiki teachers.
- Journey to meet a power animal to bring back power for your practice.
- Journey to meet a plant ally to help you connect with the wisdom of nature.
- Journey to receive healing or guidance for a specific issue.

To Drum or Not to Drum

When I first learned to journey my practice was pretty limited. I didn't have a drum and had no idea how to get hold of one. I only had a recording of a drumming on a CD that my teacher had given me so that I could practise. I used to religiously lie down in my prepared space and cover my eyes so that I could fully tune out of the real world and tune in to the shamanic worlds. I played the track to practise connecting to my guides and travelling the different worlds. This was valuable practice for me considering how unfocused I was about my intention. However, when I learned the reiki drum technique I was presented with my very first drum and I felt the power of drumming for myself, which was a game-changer. You will experience for yourself the difference between drumming for yourself, having a friend drum for you or listening to a pre-recorded track that either you or another practitioner has recorded. Neither experience is better than the other; they each have their merits and I find each of them quite different.

To learn the basics of the shamanic journeying technique you may find that it's easier to listen to a drumming track because you aren't concerned with the actual mechanics of drumming; you simply have to lie down and receive the pre-recorded sound. I often do this if I am feeling tired as I find it a relaxing way to connect to guides and receive the information or healing that I am seeking. And since you are not drumming, you can also give yourself a self-reiki treatment during the session.

If you have a trusted friend who you can pair up with to exchange drumming sessions then this is ideal, as they can hold space for you while you journey and you can do the same for them. This live drumming has a different quality to a recorded track and you will be able to become physically immersed in the vibrant sound of the drum, while at the same time your friend may also receive information on your behalf that will help you. As above, you can also give yourself reiki during the session and/or your friend can give you reiki too.

Another experience altogether is drumming for yourself and taking yourself on a drumming journey to meet your guides and seek your required information. Unlike the other two options, which feel more passive as you are simply receiving the drum, drumming for yourself is more involved and more active. It's a full-on experience for all of your senses; as well as experiencing the journeying you are responsible for the drumming that takes you there. This is why, for some beginners, it can be easier to learn the journeying technique from a drumming track, because there is less to think about. However, there is so much power in picking up your drum and allowing it to guide you that I highly recommend immersing yourself in the beat of your drum. You will learn more when you allow the drum to guide you. You may find as you drum that, naturally, the beat shifts and changes or your hand seems to falter and the beat slows.

When I drum and journey for myself my journeys are more of a felt sensation throughout the whole of my being, because there is a lot of movement as I drum. This is a different experience for me than if I lie down to simply receive the drumbeat that someone else is playing. If you struggle with the journeying process and opening up all of your senses to the rhythm of the drum, it may help you to drum for yourself to truly embody the shift in consciousness and revelations that the journey state offers.

Tips for Your Shamanic Reiki Journeys

Just to recap, there is no wrong way to journey! Don't get hung up on the structure. The key is your intention. Be open to guidance. The following tips will help you stay focused and enjoy successful journeys.

- Keep things simple at the start and create a clear intention. Write it down to help you stay focused.
- Always prepare yourself and your space appropriately – invite reiki to flow!
- Allow yourself space and time to prepare for, experience and integrate the journey in a relaxed way; it's hard to remain open and allow a journey to unfold if you feel pressed for time. Experiment with longer journeys while you get used to the process.
- Release your expectations – let go of the idea that the journey is something exotic and let it unfurl organically, almost mundanely.

- Release your impressions of what you think you should be experiencing or what the process should feel like.
- Always journey with a guide or spirit helper with you so you have a trusted ally in the other worlds who can show you what you need to know and protect you. (If you don't have a guide, make this your first journey – see below.)
- Let go of control, stay light-hearted, be curious and don't try too hard! (You might find that spirit has a sense of humour!)
- Allow the drum or the sound to move through you and move you.
- Trust you are doing it properly! – there is no correct way.
- Let go of the idea that you are simply making it all up.
- Remember to receive and open all of your senses to receive information – this is not simply a movie that you watch.
- Treat everything you receive as information, signposts and guidance.
- Always say thank you when the journey comes to an end and be clear that the experience has finished.
- Always allow time to ground yourself and integrate your experiences. For example, take a walk in nature.
- Make notes and always implement and honour any teaching, wisdom or guidance that you are given. Ask yourself, "How does this experience answer my question/intention?"

Common Pitfalls and How to Move past Them

Nothing happens

Sometimes you might feel stuck or think that nothing is happening. If you think nothing is happening, then tune in to what is in that nothingness. Record your experiences and impressions of the nothingness and feel your way into it. If you are experiencing feeling stuck and not getting anywhere, reflect on whether that in itself could be showing you something related to your journey's intention.

Feeling anxious or afraid

Be kind to yourself, remember your intention and that you can call in help. When you journey, you are in an expanded state of consciousness and you are accessing those hidden parts of yourself. If you are feeling frightened it may be that you are experiencing something that you are trying to push away from and which indicates a part of you that requires healing, love and compassion.

Ask yourself what you think the anxiety or fear is about. Remember you have helpers – ask them to come forwards. Also, your reiki practice or other reiki colleagues can provide healing. You can even take a torch with you during a journey to help shine the light in the dark and illuminate the shadows.

Being in a rush

This can stop you from truly relaxing so you stay in your mind rather than shift into a different state of consciousness. Take time to breathe slowly, relax or meditate before beginning your journey.

Feeling a time pressure during the journey

If you are not familiar with the journey process or are using a drumming track to journey with that you haven't used before, you may not relax entirely to fully experience the journey because you may feel concerned about how much time you have or when you have to return. To help you with this, use drumming tracks with which you are familiar, or if friends are drumming for you clarify timings and drumming signals with them, to indicate different phases of the journey to guide you. The best drumming tracks are always those that you record for yourself!

Getting distracted

When I first started to journey, boy did I forget to focus! I felt so relieved to have "made it" into the shamanic worlds that my excitement and general awe got the better of me. I would swiftly forget my intention for the journey and go off on tangents, marvelling at the sights and sounds of the landscape that was before me. I remember one of my first shamanic teachers reminding me to stay focused. I am still learning!

I'm making this up

You may find it much easier than you had thought it would be to slip into an altered state and therefore you may feel that you are making up the whole experience from your imagination. Does this make your experience any less valid? Could you accept that you might be able to do this easily, innately?

My guides aren't communicating with me

What makes you think this? Reflect on how open you are to receiving in general and invite reiki to help you. Where could you open to receive a little more? Pay attention to all of your senses; guides communicate in mysterious ways.

You keep falling asleep

Keep trying: experiment with journeying at different times of day when you have more energy, or drum for yourself rather than lying down to listen to a drumming track.

Trouble meeting a guide

Keep practising and exploring with this as your intention. Be proactive, rather than waiting for a guide to come to you. Keep an eye out for synchronicities and what is getting your attention, in your waking life or your dreams.

Not understanding the journey

Make notes of significant events, guidance, sensations and feelings. Don't try to analyze these during the journey or even afterwards, because during the journey your brain is in a different state. Keep all your notes and look over them for patterns. If things don't make sense immediately, give it time and come back to your notebooks later. You will find they contain gold!

Analyzing during the journey and overthinking

Remember to stay in a state of childlike curiosity during the journey. In the journey experience your brainwaves are not following the same pattens as when you are in a normal waking state, so attempting to give reason to things isn't going to work. Such a journey is an opportunity to explore with wonder and curiosity like a child. Observe, experience and partake in the adventure rather than analyze and try to find meaning with your mind. After the journey, when you are remembering the experience and noting down what feels significant, is the time for reflection, looking for familiar patterns and finding meaning with your mind.

Thinking that if you are not a visual person you can't journey properly

The journey is a process of direct revelation, which means information is shown to you directly. It isn't like a movie that you might watch; you experience it with the whole of your being. During the journey process you receive information with all of your senses. You may receive physical sensations in your body or feel states of bliss or deep emotional release. Some people are also highly susceptible to smell or specific sound frequencies that offer them information. This is why journeying to experience for yourself can feel so much richer than when others journey on our behalf.

Exploring Reiki in a Drumming Journey

When you feel more confident with the shamanic journey process you can explore how it feels to offer reiki to a person, situation, tree, animal, or even yourself or a past experience as part of the journey process. During a shamanic reiki journey you can give reiki and ask to be shown where reiki is needed, what it is doing and how it is helping. Working with reiki in the shamanic realms will be covered as part of distance healing and in the following chapter on personal healing.

Other Ways of Journeying to Practise

Since this book is about the drum, I am focusing on its part in the journey process along with reiki. However, this is not the only way to achieve an altered state of consciousness or connect with guides to receive healing and guidance. You may feel guided to explore with other methods, such as:

- Automatic writing
- Self-reiki practice, chanting and meditation with or without the symbols
- Intuitive walking in nature
- Watching for omens and signs
- Dream interpretation
- Plant medicines or plant meditations
- Working with other sound instruments or dancing

Taking Action and Honouring Your Experiences

Once you get the hang of the journeying process it will become second nature to you, like inviting reiki to flow. It can be a marvellous and yet often frustrating experience as your guides reveal information to you in curious ways that might not quite make sense at the time, or even years later! Each time you journey and enter an altered state of consciousness, you are accessing valuable information, even though it may not always feel that way. Which is why noting down whatever you experience is a key part of the process; the secrets may be revealed later on. It is important to honour the journey experience and take action to help create change in your life. After all, why are you doing this if you don't want to transform your life or become more aligned with your true nature, path and purpose here? After a journey and the integration process, ask yourself, *"What action am I now going to take in my life because of what has been revealed to me during the journey?"* Ask yourself how you can integrate this information or feeling into your life, how things can change. Nothing will change if you don't take action. Maybe you need to change the way you think about a certain part of your life or person. Maybe you need to stop doing a certain behaviour, or take better care of yourself by drinking more water. Maybe you need to start spending more time listening to your inner guidance rather than turning to others. You may find that if you are journeying, connecting with guides and not taking action, then life will not change for you. Your connection with your guides may fade over time if your relationship is not nurtured or their guidance not honoured. The action needs to come from you. One baby step at a time.

TAKE A BEAT

The journey is precisely that. It's not a process that you try once. It is a practice, a magnificent journey into the greater parts of yourself and all that connects us. You will come back to it again and again as part of reclaiming your power and your truth. Your reiki practice can be the perfect container for support and nurture as you grow. In the following chapter I'm going to share more techniques that will not only help you bond with your drum and your guides but also lead you into deeper healing pathways and spiritual evolution.

4

Personal Healing
Restoring Power

@ @ @ @

You can feel the power of the drum when you pick it up and strike a beat. When the rhythm seeps into your bones and touches your heart, this is when you remember the depths of this ancient sound and the power it has to create change within your being. I recommend that you make journeying part of your regular practice, not only to hone the technique, meet guides, receive healing and find out information but for the pure joy of drumming! As a reiki healer and lightworker, looking after your own physical, mental and emotional well-being is key to maintaining your frequency as a clear and strong channel for reiki. This chapter is going to focus on specific techniques for releasing old patterns, restoring your power and helping you align with and maintain the truth of who you are. You will also discover what a powerful instrument the drum is for shifting your mindset and bringing momentum and power to manifesting goals and dreams.

Trapped Summer, 2021

Inside my voice is trapped a secret song
A song I used to sing
When my soul was free
When was that?
Oh, so long ago I do not know.
The song isn't forgotten, just trapped.
Trapped and tapping on the walls of my throat like a dancer
  in the wings waiting to get onto the stage.
Like a horse at the starting gate.
So sing, I hear you cry.
I'm afraid, you know.
I'm afraid that when I sing again the frequency will shatter
  the world I have created and illuminate my truth for all
  to see.

The light would be unbearable!
Blinding, undeniable.
What a secret to let loose.
What a bomb to drop and devastate ignorant minds,
Zombies in human clothing.
I can't do it (yet!)
But I know I must
For I won't sleep until the very last note of my song resonates
    throughout the world I know and beyond.
For then, I will feel whole.
We will feel whole.
And then we will begin to live.

Releasing in Order to Receive

As part of my reiki and qigong energy practices I have learned the value of releasing stagnant or sluggish energy that is clogging up my energy field. You may have noticed during your reiki self-practice that, when you clear your energy field or energy centres (chakras), you can more easily receive what is available to you. Most of us have overly packed schedules and bounce from one activity to the next, constantly in demand by others either physically or via our mobile device. We have to make time to relax, reflect and even allow ourselves to get bored. Energetically we are full to the brim, which is why practices like qigong, reiki, yoga and meditation are so valuable for our mental, emotional and physical well-being.

An analogy I often give my clients is that they are walking around with their hands full, carrying heavy shopping bags. If I were to approach them offering a suitcase full of five million pounds, in order to reach out and receive it they would have to let go of what they are holding and put out an empty hand. Energetically it is the same. In order to receive what is already there or might be available to you, you have to release what you are holding onto. This might be old habits or thought patterns that no longer serve you, decisions that you are unable to make, attachments to places, events or people that don't feel healthy, expectations, anxiety about the future, judgements, and so on.

Often, we aren't even aware of how much we are holding or how it might be blocking our ability to receive. One of the first steps towards creating a life that is in alignment with your truth and with feeling like you are on your path is to release and let go of that which no longer serves you. There are many ways that you can do this with means such as energy practices, breathwork and plant medicine.

The following is a fun way to release the old, and drum and shake your way into a new frequency.

TAKE ACTION Bone Dance

This fun exercise is based on a shamanic technique of this name. The dance is a shamanic dismemberment process in which you dance and shake to dismember your physical body, including skin, hair, muscles, organs, everything except the bones. You dance as a skeleton, completely stripped of everything physical. Then the drumbeat shifts and you begin to re-member your physical body, returning all the pieces that are necessary; only this time your body is created free of all the old patterns and energetic imprints. Your body is now a clear channel, ready to receive guidance and wisdom for your highest goal as part of your spiritual journey.

Give it a try!

Begin in a space that has been prepared and feel yourself surrounded by your helping spirits with reiki flowing. Pick up your drum and connect to it with the symbols or simply with your intention.

Hold in your heart the intention to release that which no longer serves you: thought patterns, beliefs and stories, attachments, pain, and so on. Stand with your feet hip-width apart, consciously activating the bubbling spring point on the soles of your feet to connect you with the Earth. Soften throughout your body and relax. When you feel ready to begin, start to drum. As you drum, move your body to the drumbeat. The emphasis is down, down, down as if you are releasing into the Earth for the Earth to transmute the energy.

You may call in a guide to help you and ask to be shown what there is to release. Feel yourself stripping away your skin, muscles, organs and hair, sense yourself becoming lighter and free. Keep moving, bobbing and shaking parts of your body to release into the Earth.

When the time feels right (or you are guided), change the drumbeat and begin to dance yourself back together with the intention of being in alignment with your highest vibration and authentic self. Make this playful, it can be a joyful process. You may even find yourself singing and sounding as you call yourself back home. When you feel complete, put down your drum and place your hands on your heart. Breathe into this new you that has been reassembled. Feel yourself shining with the frequency that is your truth. Know yourself to be a clear channel for reiki and for your soul calling.

Play a piece of uplifting music to integrate this, or head out into nature to place your hands and feet onto the Earth or a tree to feel the aliveness of the natural world. After 5–10 minutes, make notes on the experience and how you feel now. Do you feel you have let go of something significant? How can you anchor this feeling of aliveness and alignment into your being? What might help you do this? What do you feel ready for now?

Protecting Your Frequency

The more reiki you practise and healing work that you undertake, the brighter your light that shines out into the world. This will be attractive for many beings seeking help or who are simply curious. To make sure that you feel safe, as well as have clear boundaries (which will be discussed in more detail in Chapter 8), it is helpful and reassuring to work with a guide who is specifically there to provides you with protection by helping your energy stay clear and true. A guide that sees your clear light and helps you shine at all times.

You may already have a guide whose sole purpose is to protect you, or you may feel confident in inviting reiki to protect your energy body. Even if you already have a protector guide or work in this way with reiki, I invite you to journey again to connect with the guide to find out more about how they work. If you have not previously met or asked to meet a guide who will act as your protector, then follow the guidance outlined in the "Take Action" exercise on meeting a guide on, page 67.

Have as your intention to meet a guide who will provide you with protection whenever you require it. Ask the guide questions such as:

Why are you here to protect me?

What can you see that can be cleared for me?

How do you keep my energy clear and how does that work?

My Baobab Protector

I am lucky enough to have several guides who work in this way to protect me as I connect to the shamanic realms. The first one that I met after doing a journey like this as part of my shamanic training appeared to me as a vibrant image of a tree with feathers and bells attached. It confused me and it didn't seem clear, so I journeyed again and persevered. The next time I repeated the journey, the same feeling was there but I had the sense of a male tribal warrior, though I didn't receive a name. I received the impression that in order for him to protect me I simply needed to call to him and put him around me. He seemed pretty powerful, so I was happy enough. I worked with him in this way, placing him around me, for my subsequent journeys and drumming practice.

The more I did this, the more I felt an awareness of an enormous baobab tree. It took me a while to realize that this baobab tree (which I simply need to jump inside for protection) is my guide, who acts as my protector. The warrior was the tree showing itself to me in human form so that I would accept it more easily as a guide.

These days, it is rare that I see the human form of my guide; when I call upon him he shows his true form of baobab tree to me and I dive inside.

Your Thoughts Become Things

Twenty years ago I went to a talk by Mike Dooley and his words changed my life for ever. He said that "*Thoughts become things, choose the good ones.*" What a wonderful piece of advice for someone whose mindset was at the time focused on the glass being half empty. I wasn't happy in my job, I wasn't very confident, nothing felt like it was going well and I was feeling a little lost. My vibration was low and all the negative chatter in my head was keeping it there and preventing me from accessing the abundance and love of the universe. These days, this concept is common and familiar to most of us. You can probably see how constantly telling the story of "*life isn't going that well*" was perpetuating my issues at work and general unhappiness.

Each of us carries a story around with us and over time we have become so used to our personal story that we think it's the truth. We have forgotten that we are divine beings who can create anything and everything we ever dream of and are worthy of having it all.

One of the roles of a practitioner is to empower their clients, to help them overcome blocks, fears and resistance that are preventing them from being truly in their power and shining their light out into the world. Some clients may have a story that is easy to spot: they have an illness, are in an abusive relationship, an unhappy career environment, or have a stressful life, money worries and so forth. Or they believe that they are not good enough, or unlovable. It's often much easier to spot these stories in others than it is in yourself, but it's imperative for your personal growth and healing path.

You are a creative being, and your powerful thoughts become things and experiences. Each and every thing that exists in your world was once a thought, such as your phone, car, pair of shoes, even your lip gloss.

With this in mind, pay careful attention to the story that you tell yourself about your life.

TAKE ACTION Spot the Stories and Patterns You Are Living

You are the hero of your own story, so how does your story currently go? Note it down. If it was a movie, would it seem like a fun adventure in which the hero was having an incredible time? If not, what would you change?

Sometimes the stories that we have are beautiful and full of love, success and joy. Other times we find ourselves holding on to stories that are outdated, not actually true and no longer serving us. Think of the stories that you tell yourself, the mindset that you have conditioned yourself into, the way that you react to things or feel about certain aspects of your life. Many of us have a money story, especially when it comes to earning money with our talents or holistic healing gifts. You might tell yourself that you shouldn't earn money with reiki or that you can't earn enough money working for yourself.

Think about what story you tell yourself and choose one thing that you are ready to shift and open to a new way of thinking about. You can work with this story using the technique that I share later in this chapter.

Note down what thoughts you have that may be limiting your happiness. Do you tell yourself you can't do certain things? Or don't know how? Or don't have the experience? Or that certain things are impossible for you, out of your reach, or never going to happen? Pay attention to the voice inside your head that may be judging you or putting you down on a daily basis. Many of us have a voice that tells us things like:

I am not good enough
I am not worthy of love or success
I'm not meant to be rich

I'm never going to be able to do that
I don't know what I want to do with my life

Do you tell yourself that parking for the concert will be difficult, that you'll never get a spot, and the traffic will be awful? Or do you see yourself getting a parking space with ease and traffic flowing easily?

Start to become aware of how your thoughts are influencing your feelings and be willing to change them.

You can connect with the power of reiki and the drum to help change your thought patterns with a new positive affirmation to help create the change that you desire in your life. This can be especially useful if you have a negative habit that you wish to let go of, such as emotional eating, worrying or smoking. For many it will be more of an emotional and mental habit, a way of thinking, a mindset that you have that is not serving you. You may in the previous "Take Action" exercise have identified a negative story that is on repeat and which you wish to change.

TAKE ACTION Create a New Story

This drumming process connects to the subconscious with reiki and can be used to help you or clients overcome negative habits and to focus the mind on something positive to manifest. The drum and reiki travel to the cause of where this negative pattern took root and connect this part to the vibratory consciousness of the universe to help remove the pattern. This technique is based on a technique called the Emotional Mindset Reprogramming Technique, which is taught as part of reiki drum training.

Here's how it works:

Phase 1

- As with previous exercises, prepare yourself and your space in your way. Invite in your guides and helpers and ask reiki to flow. Scribe your symbols on to your drum.
- Decide what you most need to heal or create in this current moment.
- Develop a simple affirmation to focus on for the drumming. State this affirmation in a positive sense and the present tense, as if it is already happening, and write it down.

- For example, *rather than I will stop smoking. I make healthy choices for my body.*
- Or *instead of I don't know what to do with my life. My life purpose is clear.*
- *Working for myself as a reiki practitioner is easy. It's the best-paid job I've ever had, rather than stating It's hard to earn money to support myself as a reiki practitioner.*

Phase 2

- Focus on your affirmation and begin to drum, with reiki flowing and your guides with you to assist you.
- You may feel guided to chant or visualize the reiki symbols. For example, the connection symbol (*HSZSN*) can assist with connecting to the original cause of this negative thought or unhealthy habit. The harmony symbol may be useful to help support the emotions that are connected to this negative pattern and the power symbol (*CKR*) will empower the affirmation.
- You may like to chant your affirmation as you drum.
- Drum for 10–20 minutes, allowing yourself to truly embrace and open to the resonance of your affirmation.
- When you feel the session is complete, put down your drum and give yourself a self-treatment with reiki for around 10–15 minutes or as long as you wish.
- Give thanks to reiki, your guides and the drum and close your space in your usual way, intending that the session is complete.

Phase 3

- Make sure you feel grounded; go out into nature if possible, and have a drink of water.
- Reflect on your experience and how you feel about the affirmation now. It may have shifted into something else, so feel into this. Ask yourself how you can integrate this experience and commit to one step that you can make to create change in your life.
- Repeat this once a week for the next three weeks and review your affirmation at the end of the month.
- Notice what has shifted about how you feel about the issue. Adjust the affirmation accordingly.

- You may wish to play a drumming track and give yourself a self-reiki treatment instead of drumming for yourself here. Experiment to see what feels more powerful or comfortable for you.

Affirmation Suggestions

These can be used with your personal practice or to help clients:

- I am enough
- I am so grateful for my life
- Everything is always working out for me
- I am worthy of love
- I feel supported and loved in my work and at home
- I am full of joy for life's adventure
- I am open to receiving new opportunities
- My body is healthy and pain-free
- Working for myself is easy; it's the best job I've ever had
- My needs are always abundantly met
- I accept myself and love myself deeply
- I trust myself and feel guided clearly by my inner wisdom
- I am blessed with an incredible family and amazing friends

Shifting Your Frequency

You will no doubt be familiar with the law of attraction that shows us that *"energy flows where your attention goes"*. This means that if we want to attract good things, we need to focus on what is already good in our lives rather than highlighting the negative. I find the Abraham-Hicks affirmations like *"Things are always working out for me"* really useful to help keep the energy flow feeling open to opportunity rather than shut down.

In order to help you shift your frequency, it is helpful to remind yourself of people, places, things, activities or music that bring you joy and make your heart sing. Don't simply make a list of these things, actively seek them out in your daily life to be in their frequency. Cultivate radiance by sensing their quality and vibration. See if you can match it and find those qualities within yourself.

For example, if the sound of children giggling makes your heart sing, notice how you feel when you hear this sound. Notice what effect it has on your body, thoughts, and feelings. Sense into the quality of the energy of it and find this quality within you to radiate back. Remember that you are a vibration of light.

Transfiguration is a shamanic technique that involves shape-shifting and tapping into the light and love within you and radiating this out into the world. This not only shifts your frequency but transforms and raises the vibration of those around you. When we invite reiki to flow, we are in this transfigured state as the light and love of reiki becomes us (reminds us who we truly are), affects our energy field, and naturally changes the frequency that we radiate.

`TAKE ACTION` Drumming Your Radiant (Reiki) Self

If it appeals to you, then invite reiki to flow and pick up your drum. Your intention is to drum and connect with reiki together with the energy of those things that bring you joy, and feel the vibration of it. You may find this quite a blissful experience.

Meet a guide as you drum and ask to be shown how to access the radiance within yourself and help it to grow.

When you feel ready stop drumming, integrate the experience, ground yourself, and journal on what you have learned. Notice how this way of being your radiant (reiki) self may be transforming your family, friends, and colleagues around you. You can also practise this with the intention to heal specific places, particularly those affected by environmental pollution.

Reclaiming Your Power

When you are fully aligned and holding your power, there is nothing in this world that is more powerful than the magical divine being that you are. Power restoration or power retrieval is an essential shamanic practice that calls back power that you may have given away or may have been taken from you, in this life and beyond. Power loss is common for everyone, but it is certainly more visible in people who are depressed, or follow patterns of chronic illness or misfortune, or are victims of abusive relationships, for example, or bullied at school and then later bullied in the workplace. Power loss can also be more subtle. It happens when you feel overwhelmed at work, weighed down by burdens, unable to speak up for yourself, overpowered or powerless, or suffer trauma. For me, my pattern was connected to giving my power away to authority; this may have started in my early years but it continued into adulthood and it wasn't serving me. I was giving my power away to those who I perceived to be in a position of authority and this behaviour meant I was allowing myself to be controlled by others unnecessarily.

Typical symptoms of power loss are: feeling depressed or unmotivated, illness, lacking in energy and motivation, feeling lost or lacking in creativity. Because power loss is so common and the pattern repeats itself, when calling back your power it's beneficial to go back to the original source of power loss. This could even be in another lifetime.

SELF-REFLECTION   What Does Power Mean to You?

- What makes you feel powerful?
- Where do you give your power away?
- Have you ever felt that your power was taken from you?

You may have heard of the term "Power animal". This refers to an animal spirit guide who appears to bring back your power as part of a healing journey. Don't get impatient, you're going to do this shortly! When I first started my shamanic path, I used to get slightly irritated by people frequently asking me, "What's your power animal?" I felt as if people thought shamanism was just about having a power animal and had no idea about the wealth of other healing practices and guides that it involves. I also felt that I didn't want to share the special connections I have with my animal totems. However, maybe people get rather fixated on having a power animal because it's such an important part of you to reconnect with.

One of the very first animals that I met as part of a drumming journey to meet a power animal was during my reiki drum training with Sarah Gregg in 2009. As Sarah drummed we journeyed and I met with two snakes, each with very distinctive markings. The snakes held me down so that I could not escape the healing and transformation that was occurring. They also shared some information with me to help me on my path. For a while this pair accompanied me on my journeys, but I rarely see them now. I have other guides that connect with me at this time: animals, trees, humans and birds.

When you have your personal power restored following a shamanic healing, you may feel a sense of wonder and as if you are more deeply connected to yourself and your purpose in life. The healing process brings back life force energy for you and this also helps you feel more motivated, energized and able to heal and move through life with ease. Are you ready?

TAKE ACTION Journey to Restore Power

Prepare your space and yourself to journey as you have many times before. Note down your intention: "I intend to restore my power and meet a power animal."

You may like to listen to a drumming track to fully receive this, or you may feel more excited to drum for yourself. These instructions are for you to follow if you are drumming for yourself. If you are listening to a drumming track then you can place your hands on or over your body for the duration to experience self-reiki.

Pick up your drum and call to you a guide to help you travel into the lower world. Drum and feel yourself in your special place in nature, travelling down into the Earth. Use the reiki symbols to connect you to the lower world.

When you feel you have arrived in the lower world, ask your guide to help you restore your power. You may see animals, so be aware of what you are seeing as you move around in the lower worlds. Notice the landscape that you are in. You may be in forest, desert, a meadow, in the mountains or by a river. Notice which animals are appearing to you. Be particularly aware of any animal that shows itself to you several times. You can ask it – are you here to bring my power back? Keep drumming, noticing how you feel both in your body and emotionally. Allow the journey to play out with the beat of the drum. Imagine that each drumbeat is bringing you closer to your power animal, connecting you with its frequency – that is, the resonance of your power. Receive this with the whole of your being. You may find yourself merging with the animal and making specific movements as the energy of the animal connects with yours. Enjoy this sacred dance and feel the animal come alive within you!

When the time feels right, return to your world by retracing your steps. Place your hands over your heart to breathe in the power of the animal. Hold your hands there to fully receive for as long as feels right. You may also like to play your integration music, or simply sit and receive in silence.

As you are receiving, ask for further guidance. Notice what you can sense from this frequency. What qualities does this have for you? How can this help you? When you feel complete, make sure you are grounded and fully back in your physical body.

Journal on your thoughts and feelings. You may even like to practise some automatic writing, asking the animal what qualities it is bringing to help you and what it can help you with.

Reflect on what this animal and connection mean to you. How does this make you feel? What might change now because of this? And how can you keep this connection strong?

How can you honour your animal guide?

To complete, thank your guides and close your space.

Rather than rush to look up what this particular animal means as depicted by someone else, reflect on what it means for you. Of course it is useful to find out about the physical nature of the animal, but make sure you ask your animal about its unique connection with you rather than rely solely on other texts that may not carry meaning for you.

Some practitioners honour their animal totems and remember this connection by, for example, carrying a picture or item depicting the animal on their person or on display in their sacred space.

Remember you can, and would be wise to, journey again to connect with your animal guide to find out more about it and the qualities that it is returning to you. It may be happy in the background or it may be here for a specific mission. Find out, and take action accordingly. You may feel guided to decorate or paint your drum with a specific animal to honour your guide.

TAKE ACTION Reclaiming Your Voice

Your voice is one of the most powerful tools that you have for healing and shaping the world, and yet so many of us have been shut down at some stage in our life and are afraid to speak out. Are you someone who is easily able to speak up and share your point of view? Are there times in your life where you have not been able to make yourself heard? Is there something within you that needs expressing yet feels stuck in your body?

Being able to express what we hold inside helps our vital force to flow. When this is stuck, imbalances can be felt across mind, body and spirit and this loss of power can be devastating.

The following practice can help transform a past experience that feels lodged in the body into sound that moves though you, with reiki and your drum to support the process. You are also going to call on your winged friends as allies to help free your voice and help your expressive nature to fly. You may like to do this outside where you can be in the presence of birds and hear their song.

Prepare yourself and your space and call in reiki, your guides and helpers. Also invite in the birds to bring their voices and sense of freedom into your healing space. Connect with your drum and charge it with your intention, which is to free and release your voice and to reclaim its power. If there is a specific moment in time that you feel called to heal, then add this to your intention. Make use of the distance/connection symbol to help you.

Begin to drum with the symbols to locate any pain or stuck energy. Notice where in your body you feel this. Trust that your body knows.

With the drum to support you, start to give voice to this energy. You may feel a small bubbling up at first; simply allow whatever sounds to come out of you.

Let yourself express this energy with sounds and movements that support you and feel right. Allow it to move out of you.

Continue drumming and sounding until you feel complete. Put down your drum and place your hands over areas of your body that you feel drawn to. Self-treat with reiki for 5–10 minutes, then give thanks and close down your space.

Notice how you feel now and write about your experiences. What has shifted?

Charging Your Goals and Vision with Reiki and the Drum

I drifted through my twenties taking opportunities that came up here and there and going with the flow. Unlike many of my friends, I never knew what I wanted to do. This suited me – or so I thought; deep down I felt lost. With the encouragement of reiki, the hidden parts of myself started to come out and play and I allowed myself to gravitate more to those things that lit me up (like plants and healing). With the addition of the drum to my practice, a renewed sense of creativity was born that enabled me to grow beyond the small box that I had allowed myself to be placed into. Along with the sense of connectivity that the drum generated, it gifted me with an expanded sense of vision. I began to realize that I could shape my life with intention, choices and focus. The world was a much more magical place when I expanded my vision. It was empowering for me to remember that we are all creative beings, and I no longer pushed my dreams and wishes away.

What is it that you long to create for yourself and for others? If this question leaves you in a place of "I don't know", then compassionately offer yourself reiki. Create a safe environment for yourself to explore the "I don't know", and imagine – What if I did know?

If the question inspired you to list off those longings that you hold, then pick one for this drum practical below. Reiki and the drum powerfully combine to bring momentum to our goals and visions, as well as bringing in inspiration and assistance from the other realms.

TAKE ACTION Drumming to Manifest a Goal

1. Invite reiki to flow through you and call in your guides and helpers for assistance.
2. Connect with a project or goal that you would like to achieve or a vision for your life that you desire to realize. Invoke the distance symbol *HSZSN* (connection) to help you connect.
3. Visualize the positive outcome that you desire and bring it to life in your inner vision. Create a beautiful picture of this in your mind and your heart.
4. Bring your vision to life with feelings, words, symbols and pictures. Sense into how it would feel to be living this vision or achieving this goal. What does it look like in your daily life? What conversations do you picture yourself having? What clothes are you wearing? Who are you hanging out with? Who is emailing you? What are they saying? What are you doing on a day-to-day basis? What difference are you making in the world because of this amazing achievement? Feel yourself achieving this dream or goal. Tune in to what that would feel like, how that would change your life; make it come alive with sounds, colour, images as if it was truly happening now. Make this as vivid as possible, as if you were watching or experiencing a movie. It might help to imagine a conversation in which you might be telling your friends and family that you have achieved this. For example, imagine telling a friend you are moving to the most

sought-after neighbourhood in your area. Feel your excitement and hear their reaction. Or if your goal is to get fit, for example, you might imagine yourself wearing different clothes, feeling more confident in your body and hearing people around you compliment your toned physique. Explore this and have fun! Bring your vision to life with as many of your senses as you can, as vividly as you can.

5. When you feel ready, pick up your drum and charge it with the reiki symbols to help you connect to the energy of your vision. Invite reiki and the drum to help you release what blocks you.

6. Drum for as long as you feel guided, working intuitively or with the symbols to bring power to your vision and remove obstacles in your way. You may also wish to ask for something specific, like guidance or healing, to help you move towards this vision (or something better!) freely and swiftly for the highest good of all beings.

7. Be open to what you may experience in your body, your mind and emotions. You may receive images, information, thoughts, feelings, ideas, memories, songs, names or whatever flows!

8. Release your expectations and just allow the drum to play through you.

9. When the drumming feels complete, give thanks and close down your space. Allow yourself time to integrate the experience by going out into nature to connect with the land or listening to a favourite piece of music.

10. Journal on what this journey felt like, what feels significant and what you have learned.

11. Ask yourself, what is one step that you can take today towards this vision?

12. What needs to happen next for you to bring this goal or vision closer?

13. What tools do you already have that you can work with to help you further? (hint – reiki!) Make sure you take action on any guidance provided by your helpers and keep focusing on your goal. Revisit this journey to ask for guidance that will help support your vision and notice how it shifts.

Drumming Tracks for Personal Healing

One of my favourite ways to self-treat with reiki is at night, in bed before I go to sleep. Most nights I place my hands over areas of my body that need care and attention and invite reiki to flow. It is a great comfort to feel the warm blanket of reiki flowing to where it is needed. The disadvantage of the drum is that you cannot totally relax to receive healing like this if you are playing the drum yourself. The answer is to either buddy up with a friend who can drum for you or to record a drumming track for yourself.

You can record a drumming track for a general intention such as "to help you relax, let go of tension and feel balanced in your body, mind and spirit" or for a more specific ailment that requires healing. You can also record specific drumming tracks that will take you on a shamanic journey to help you access information from your spirit guides and allow you to explore the shamanic universe. If this is something that appeals to you, recording healing drumming tracks for clients may be a service that you are willing to offer.

TAKE ACTION Record a Drumming Track

Create your sacred space, decide on your intention and work out your tech. The easiest way to record a drumming track is to use a voice recorder, which most mobile devices have. Alternatively you may like to set up a microphone and use a program such as Audacity that has a much wider range of features and will most likely achieve a higher-quality recording.

Do a sound check before you start so that you know the range of sound that your recording device can pick up without distorting and understand how far to position yourself away from the microphone or device.

Connect to reiki and your drum. You may like to spend a while in *gassho* feeling into your intention. As part of your intention you will add *"May I receive the healing that I need now and whenever I listen to the drumming track, for the highest good of all beings."*

When you feel ready press start on your tech, say the intention for the drumming or journey and start your drumming, holding in your heart your intention. Use the symbols as you feel guided and enjoy the process. Bring the drumming to a close when you feel you have done enough, and close your space in the appropriate way. Press *stop* on your recording device.

You may also like to self-treat with reiki to help you ground and integrate your experience of drumming. This recording can then be played back whenever you need it and you can self-treat with reiki while you are receiving the drum healing for additional benefits. If you have the tech available to you, you may like to include a short meditation track with music at the beginning or at the end to help complete the session.

Receiving Healing from a Drum Journey

We often journey for others to receive information or send them healing as part of our role as practitioner. We often journey for ourselves, in order to meet guides and receive insight. It can also be a wonderful experience to drum for yourself to simply RECEIVE healing. Before you begin this exercise, reflect on what you would most like healing for and create a healing intention. If you are not sure then try this diagnostic exercise.

TAKE ACTION Self-Diagnosis with the Drum

The drum can be used to locate areas of imbalance in the body and focus healing. Sometimes our discomfort is obvious, such as the physical pain of stomach cramps or a throbbing head after a day at work. However, much of the time our discomfort lies a little deeper and is more subtle, so is often overlooked until it gets worse. The drum can help tune in to the subtle frequencies of your body's orchestra and locate areas that need to be brought back into harmony.

This is easy to do, either for yourself or a client.

Take a deep breath and exhale. Invite in your guides and helpers, including reiki. Hold as your intention to do a diagnostic to find out where you most need healing now.

Play the drum when you feel centred. Don't move or sway as the drum plays (this is quite hard not to do!). Allow the drumbeat to flow through you.

Notice where in your body you sense the drumbeat most. Trust your first response.

Drum for a few more minutes, noticing any other areas of the body that are also feeling the drum.

Put the drum down and place your hands over the areas that you identified and self-treat with reiki.

You can journey again with the drum if you want further insight about the issue or simply to experience a healing journey to receive healing, as in the practical outlined below.

TAKE ACTION Drumming to Receive Healing

You could record this journey so you can play yourself a drumming track whenever you wish to receive healing for a specific issue.

In sacred space and with reiki flowing, your guides and helpers present, tune in to an area of your life or your health that would benefit from healing and needs to change.

Get clear on an intention for the journey. It can also be wonderful to invite in the presence of a healing guide, god, goddess, animal spirit, or angel to offer you that healing.

For example, if you feel aligned with Archangel Raphael, Usui himself, Mary Magdalene or Kwan Yin, invite them in to bring their healing frequency into your session.

When you feel ready, pick up your drum and see yourself in your special place in nature. You may find that for healing purposes, your guide takes you to a special place in the shamanic realms: a healing cave, sacred site, healing spring or other such place with specific healing qualities. If you wish to call in the presence of another god or goddess or special being then do so. Relax and allow yourself to be guided as you drum. You may find yourself naturally drumming softly if you require rest and nurture, or more vigorously if your energy field requires clearing and energizing.

You may feel guided to use the reiki symbols or sing their mantras as you drum. Allow yourself to be held by the drum and the energy. Ask your guide or the other guides present if you have specific questions about your healing issue and what you can do to heal.

When you feel ready and the healing feels complete, retrace your footsteps in your inner vision and feel yourself fully back in your physical reality. Offer thanks to the helping spirits and close down your space. Rest for ten minutes by giving yourself self-reiki and playing gentle music to bring you back round.

Make sure you are fully grounded and ready to be present in your life. Journal on your experiences and any guidance that you may have gleaned. Notice how you feel now compared to when you first began.

Experiencing Reiki in the Shamanic Realms

To experience another dimension of reiki and be shown how it assists in healing, experiment with a journey in which you offer yourself reiki. It's double the fun to lie down and self-treat with reiki while experiencing this journey and listening to a drumming track. Imagine how powerful it can be if the track you are listening to is one that you recorded specifically for you!

NOTE: This journey is different from the one in "Drumming to Receive Healing" previously. There, the idea was to receive healing and invite in assistance to offer this to you, whereas in this Take Action exercise you are sending reiki to yourself as part of the journey process. It is a more active approach and may provide you with insight about how reiki works through you and with you.

TAKE ACTION   Self-Reiki Shamanic Journey

In your sacred space, call in your helpers and reiki. Lie down and focus on your healing intention. A suggestion for a general intention could be "to offer myself reiki and receive the healing that I need most now for my highest good," though add your own specific healing requirements as needed.

Spend as long as you need quietening your mind in *gassho* and, when you feel ready, play your drumming track and place your hands comfortably on your body to self-treat with reiki.

Follow the journey process that you have already practised. For this journey, you may find yourself in the middle world, so you may feel like you are looking at yourself in a version of the space in which you are physically located. Have a guide with you to help you and show you areas of your body, emotions, mind and energy body that require healing. You may find yourself offering yourself a similar reiki treatment to that which you would offer a client in the physical reality, or it may be something entirely different. As always, allow yourself to relax and be guided. Notice what happens when reiki flows through you in the journey. Ask your guide for information to help you with your healing.

When the drumming track calls you back, you may like to spend five minutes listening to music and self-treating with reiki to integrate the experience. When you feel ready, give thanks and close down your space.

Write notes on how you feel and what you experienced in the journey. Notice what insights you now have about your health and well-being or about reiki itself.

While it is expansive and interesting to experience reiki in another dimension in this way, I am the first to admit that a process like this can overcomplicate a simple hands-on reiki self-treatment! Working with reiki in a shamanic journey is perhaps better suited to healing past situations that are still affecting you today. During the journey process you can travel back in time with guides and helpers to send reiki to yourself and those involved in the situation. This is a more active and often sensory experience than the classic process of sending reiki to a past situation, which is often taught at reiki Level 2. If it calls you to experiment then do so.

TAKE A BEAT

There are as many ways to heal and shine your authentic frequency as there are stars in the sky. Your personal pathway of development and expansion depends on your awareness, your quest for the truth, your willingness to change and your intentions to heal. As ever, there will be practices I have outlined here that do not appeal, so let those ones go. Maybe you will come back to them later if they are meant for you. Lean in to those practices that appeal to you and which you find useful. You will be shown by your guides and reiki what you need to release, embrace and accept as part of your journey towards wholeness. Be patient with yourself and be your own best friend. Keep gently working on the personal stories that you carry – and if they don't suit you, then change them!

Practical experience of the drum for your personal healing path not only strengthens your relationship with your spirit guides and experiences of the shamanic worlds but also helps build your confidence when working in the treatment space with others. In this next chapter you are going to explore how to bring the drum into your reiki practice to help clients, friends and family discover the healing secrets of the drum.

5

Drumming for Others

◎ ◎ ◎ ◎

Once you have got a feel for your drum, it's natural to want to share this unique experience with others. If you have a client base as part of your professional reiki practice there are various ways to include drumming as part of your regular offerings, which I'm going to share here in this chapter. There's also the opportunity to share drum healing and journeying as part of group gatherings and, given the wide range of options, I've dedicated a chapter to this later on. You will probably find that clients become as hooked as you are on the magic of the drumbeat.

What Happens When We Drum for a Client?

How do you explain the curious effect that the drum has on our human physiology and emotions? It may be helpful to share with clients the science around sound healing to help them understand the effects of the drum and how it can benefit them. You may also find yourself sharing your experience of shamanism to give them a broader idea of the worlds that the drumbeat can open up. It always helps clients to understand and relate to you if you can share the ways in which the drum has transformed your life. The drumbeat helps you attune to the intuitive frequency of yourself if you are drumming for yourself, or that of the client for whom you are drumming. When you drum for a client you consciously hold the intention for them to receive healing according to their needs. It's this intention that focuses you and helps you to navigate your way through the energetic field. As you drum, you may feel and sense into the unified field, rather like when you are practising reiki. You may sense patterns, energies, blocks and stories that a client (or you, if the subject is you) are holding onto or carrying. The drum can help you to find those stories or trapped negative patterns and find a way to set them free to bring the vibration back into alignment with the true vibration of the client. As you drum your senses will be heightened and guides, spirit helpers or ancestors may appear to help you. When working with the drum and reiki, you simply hold the beat of the drum with your intention and navigate the energy field to restore the connection with pure potential energy (source). Together with the drum, you and your guides are restoring wholeness and belonging.

Clearing Your Energy Field and Strengthening Your Frequency

In Chapter 3 you met some basic principles for cleansing your energy field with reiki before your personal journey work. Now, you're going to look at this from the practitioner's perspective. There are many ways to clear your or a client's energy field and call in protection before a treatment or shamanic journey to keep your frequency high.

You may already have been taught or guided to practise certain methods with symbols, guides or visualization. There are various ways to apply the power symbol (*Cho Ku Rei*), which is learned at reiki Level 2 to clear energy centres and bring in protection. This is often referred to as strengthening your light and will help you maintain a powerful authentic frequency that not only feels protective but also helps focus reiki healing.

The pointers below suggest various ways to apply the power symbol when working with a client.

METHOD 1 *(before a treatment as protection)*

FOR YOURSELF: Draw, drum or visualize a large power symbol in front of you, repeating its mantra to yourself, and step into it. Then draw, drum or visualize the symbol in each of your chakras from your root up to your crown, with the intention that each of your energy centres is *aligned with your true self, clear and open to the full power of reiki.* This strengthens your light and will not be affected by the energies of the treatment.

METHOD 2 *(before a treatment to clear a client's energy centres)*

FOR YOUR CLIENT: Draw, drum or visualize the symbol in each of your client's chakras from the root up to the crown, or however you feel called, with the intention that each of their energy centres is *aligned with their true self, clear and protected with the power of reiki.*

METHOD 3 *(at the end of a treatment to seal the treatment)*

FOR YOUR CLIENT: Repeat method two with the intention that each of the client's energy centres is *aligned with their true self, clear and protected with the power of reiki and grounded into the Earth.* You can also draw, drum or visualize a large power symbol over the client, repeating its mantra to yourself.

METHOD 4 *(for yourself at the end of a treatment)*

FOR YOURSELF: Draw, drum or visualize a large power symbol in front of you, repeating its mantra to yourself, and step into it. Then if you feel it is needed draw, drum or visualize the symbol in each of your chakras from your root up to your crown with the intention that each of your energy centres is *aligned with your true self, clear and protected by the power of reiki and grounded into the Earth.*

Introducing the Drum

Your friends and clients will be curious to find out more about the drum, especially if they have heard you talk about it or even heard you playing. As with a regular reiki session, there are several necessary steps for preparation before a treatment begins.

Together with preparing yourself and your space, it's imperative that you discuss the drum with the client beforehand if you plan to include it during a session.

If a client books a reiki treatment, they expect a reiki treatment – not the drum! Just because you enjoy the drum so much and might even feel guided to work with it for the client's benefit, that doesn't give you licence to play! Be very clear at the start of a treatment what will be involved if you are going to work with the drum.

It may also be helpful to share what the benefits of the drum are to help clients understand why it might help them.

I also like to show my drum to the client so that they can have a good look or touch if needed, and then I gently beat the drum to give them an idea of the sound. I might even play it really loudly so that they have an idea of the range and the different tones. I also demonstrate how far away from their body I will be playing the drum. Letting the client know that they can stop the drumming at any time by raising their hand or saying stop also gives reassurance that they are in charge and there is nothing to fear.

The more information you can offer the client at the start of the treatment, the more reassured they will feel and the easier it is for them to relax on the couch with an understanding of how the treatment will flow and what to expect.

Beginning a Reiki Treatment with the Drum

By taking a moment to say a prayer or invocation before beginning a treatment, you are strengthening your intent to send reiki for the highest good and surrendering to its flow. An example of such an invocation is as follows, but it can also be as simple as "Reiki On". You will know what's right for you.

> *"I invite reiki to flow through me with love, light and*
> *wisdom to provide healing for the highest good.*
> *May I be guided and protected. I call forward the reiki*
> *Masters past and present, my guides and any other beings*
> *of light to assist me in this healing."*

You will also want to charge your drum with the reiki symbols – see below.

Charging the Drum

Whether you are playing for yourself, drumming a journey for a client or a group or helping a client to relax or heal with the drum, connecting to your drum prior to beginning your healing work will help you focus. I recommend that as part of your preparation routine, you add time to connect with your drum. You can do this in any way that you feel guided.

Some practitioners will scribe the symbols onto the drum head with their dominant hand or the beater stick itself. I simply visualize the symbols and hold the drum in my hands with my hands touching the drum head. You may also like to speak the reiki principles, or simply breathe and invite reiki to flow. There are many ways and it's important to follow those that have meaning for you, rather than those that you feel you "ought" to do.

Relaxation with the Drum

One of the easiest ways to introduce a client or a friend to the drum is as a tool for relaxation. This can be particularly beneficial at the start of a treatment, since most people arrive for a reiki session carrying a lot of tension or anxiety and are very much in their head with preoccupied thoughts running wild. Drumming with long slow soft beats can help a client to relax and then you can gently speed up the rhythm to help further shift their brainwaves into a deeper relaxation.

After about 5–10 minutes, depending on how relaxed the client appears, you can stop drumming and start your reiki session as usual. You may find that in this relaxed state the client is more open to receiving reiki and can heal at a deeper level.

If you like to talk clients through a visualization to help them relax and prepare for a reiki session then you may like to do this with the background beat of your drum. Similarly, you can beat the drum and encourage the client to breathe deeply in on one beat and exhale following the next beat.

VISUALIZATION Drum and Breathe Visualization

This is an example of a relaxation technique with the drum that I use to help a client focus on their breath and become present and open to the beat of the drum.

- Invite the client to take the longest, slowest and deepest breaths that they have taken all day.
- Begin to softly beat your drum with the intention to send reiki to relax the client. Play long, slow soothing notes. With every beat of the drum, invite the client to let go of their burdens and allow the drum to carry them away.
- Inhale and receive the beat of the drum.
  Exhale and let go of the past.
- Inhale this present moment.
  Exhale and be here now.
- With every beat of the drum, invite the client to open a little more and be held by the drumbeat.
- Inhale and open.
  Exhale and relax.
- With every beat of the drum, invite the client to soften and be held by the beat of the drum.
- Inhale and receive.
  Exhale and let go.
- With every beat of the drum, invite the client to relax and invite the drum to take them on a journey.
- Inhale and be held.
  Exhale and feel free.

- Continue in this manner with soft long drumbeats and calming affirmations. When the client appears calmer suggest that they return to their own breathing rhythm which should now be slower. Begin the Drum treatment when you feel ready.

Drumming softly with reiki to help a client relax.

Drum Healing in a Reiki Session

One of the skills of a reiki practitioner is to listen to clients and open your special senses to truly understand what it is that the client needs help with. You may find that reiki helps you to do this while you are discussing the treatment at the start of the session. I always find that asking questions and listening are key.

The following guidelines are designed to show you the basic structure of working with the drum for healing in a reiki session.

STEP 1: Introduce the client to the drum, make sure they understand what the treatment involves. The client may feel the vibrations of the drum on their skin when you get physically close, so advise them ahead of time to avoid surprises.

STEP 2: Together with the client, create a healing intention for the session that they are happy with. If the client is unsure, they can simply have an intention *"to relax and receive the healing I most need right now"*.

If the client has identified an issue that they are facing, check that they are ready to release this issue and make the necessary changes in their life.

STEP 3: Remind the client that if they feel uncomfortable at any time they should let you know and you will stop drumming or drum more softly.

STEP 4: Ask the client to lie down on the couch, get comfortable and close their eyes. Of course, they can remain seated if they prefer.

STEP 5: Connect with reiki in the way that you have been taught, call on your guides and invoke the healing intention. Connect to your drum and, when you feel ready, begin as follows:

STEP 6: Assist the client in relaxation, either by sending reiki for 5–10 minutes as you would normally do or by talking them through a guided meditation with or without the drumbeat. If it's a client that I don't know well, I often play soft music and will place my hands on their body as I offer reiki because I find that this helps clients to relax.

I find that I mostly concentrate around the head and shoulders. Another way to help a client relax quickly would be to spend a few moments sending reiki over each of the energy centres, starting at the crown and going down to the root.

STEP 7: Scan the client's energy field, if you feel guided (more about scanning with the drum below), and draw a large power symbol over their body – and also over each of their energy centres.

STEP 8: Drum for a maximum of 20 minutes over the client's body and through their energy field. You will be 30–50 cm away from the client and you will drum more softly around the heart chakra and around the head and ears. Work with the reiki symbols as you feel guided. I like to work with the connection symbol to create a bridge between me and the client. If you see that the client is experiencing emotional release then you may feel guided to invoke the harmony symbol to assist you. You will have to use your common sense and gauge, depending on the acoustics of the room that you are in and your proximity to the client, how intensely or loudly to beat your drum.

Rather than turn a client over during a treatment, I often leave them to relax on their back. You may find that you wish to drum upwards underneath the treatment couch to access the back of a client's body more closely.

STEP 9: When you feel guided to stop drumming or you feel the time is up, put down your drum. Give the client reiki with hands either on or off in your usual way. I like to place my hands onto the client physically so that they know where I am and can relax and feel reassured. It's also helpful to do this if they have fallen asleep during the drumming, as the gentle pressure from your hands may wake them up. You may wish to play music to help the client relax and to integrate the healing. I often start with hands-on healing and then migrate to beaming reiki from a distance so that the session can integrate and the energy can settle.

STEP 10: After 10–20 minutes of reiki or when you feel ready, finish the treatment as you would finish a regular reiki session.

STEP 11: Make sure you give thanks to your drum, to reiki and to all the helping spirits. You can close the session with a large power symbol, and make sure you detach from the client's energy field. I like to also imagine the client in a large ball of reiki surrounding them protectively.

STEP 12: Give the client water and allow them time to come back. Depending on how long you have spent giving reiki, you may wish to play a piece of music here to give the client more integration time to receive guidance and to come back to reality. Give positive feedback accordingly and listen to their experience just as you would for a regular reiki session.

After the treatment, cleanse the space.

Scanning with the Drum

You may already have experience of scanning the energy field using reiki. Scanning with reiki is a simple and useful technique that gives you a felt sense of the energy field in your hands before a treatment. It shows you which areas of the energy field feel slightly different and may require more attention than others. I always recommend practising scanning either in your own energy field or that of clients, because it provides you with experience of how different energy fields feel and the more experience you have, the more you come to recognize differences in energy.

To scan the energy field, the simplest way is to hold your hands about 10 cm above the body and move your hands slowly down the body through the energy field. You may sense heat, tingling, cold, pulsing or even pain. Sometimes your hands may even feel magnetized to a specific area. There is a definite felt sensation using this method of scanning. You may also feel guided intuitively to work on other areas of the body. When you scan with the drum, the method is similar, only you are playing the drum through the energy field rather than simply relying on the sensation in your hands. Hold your drum about 30–50 cm away from the client and drum gently through the energy field. You can go closer to the body; however, make sure you keep your distance around the head and ears.

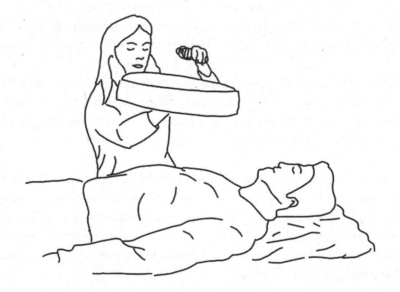

Scanning the energy field with the drum.

During this process, you are getting to know your client's energy field and tuning in to how it feels. I like to travel from the head to the feet and back up to the head again, or alternatively I may travel in a circle around the client's body from the head down one side to the feet and up one side back to the head again. As you scan, hold as your intention to be shown where the healing is needed. You might find that the drumbeat shifts slightly during this process or that it falters, so keep listening to the beat and feeling the energy field. If you would like to make this an interactive process, you can invite the client to notice where on their body they feel the drum most while you are playing and ask them to place their hands there. This will give you an indication of where they may subconsciously need healing.

Tips on Drum Technique

If you are new to drumming or are offering many treatments, you can tire easily. It helps to use your shoulder, wrist and arm with minimal effort as you drum, otherwise you may find that you get a sore wrist and won't be able to sustain long drumming sessions. Revisit Chapter 2 for other ways to hold the drum, such as cradling it in your arm or resting it on your knee. These can help if you are feeling tired, and are just as effective as holding the drum in the air. I find that switching between working with my hands and my beater to create sound helps to take the pressure off my wrist. Remember to never beat a drum in the centre; aim your beater off centre. You will discover that different types of treatment require a different approach: some will need the caring, nurturing frequency of harmony and peace and others will require power, momentum and energy. It may help to consider the yin and the yang of sound. When you make a sound with the drum, this is yang, active energy. What comes after the sound is yin, soft and restorative.

We need the balance of yin–yang to create harmony in our energy body. The space between the sounds is necessary for healing, so don't be afraid to welcome in the stillness. The moments between the beats are just as important to the healing process as the beat itself. Also remember that louder is not better. Loud sound can trigger the fight or flight response and raise the heart rate, releasing adrenaline. This may be what is needed for some clients, but not always. Allow the drum to guide you. Start softly as you get used to your client and used to your drum, and how it resonates within the space you are playing.

Finishing and Integrating a Reiki Drum Treatment

Finishing a treatment with reiki and the drum can be done in the same way as finishing a reiki session. When you feel it is appropriate to end (or time dictates), smooth down the client's aura and step away out of their energy field. A popular technique for finishing is wrapping up the client in a ball or bubble of reiki light and love to protect them and seal the healing. Always remember to say thank you, thank you, thank you to reiki, your drum and whatever else assisted you.

After a period of drumming, whether as part of a reiki treatment or a shamanic reiki drum journey, allowing ample time for quiet time, stillness and integration is a vital step of the healing process. This is where the practice of drumming differs slightly to classic reiki practice. After a reiki session we generally give the client a casual few minutes to come back from their relaxing state while we busy ourselves with offering them a glass of water or writing notes. Because the drum is such a dynamic tool that shifts energy, even a short period of drumming can instigate deep transformation, so I recommend that the integration time is longer and a structured part of the treatment. I think of a client's energy body like a snow globe that has been shaken and needs time to settle again. As the snow globe settles the landscape comes back into view and may look slightly different. In order for the client to integrate the drum experience into their whole being and bring together all of the benefits and shifts that may have taken place, they need quiet time. I play music for about ten minutes and gently remind the client that all they need to do is to lie there and be with their experience. Resist the temptation to rush this part. Allow the client to rest, settle, integrate, observe and open to receive this new shift. It helps to forewarn the client at the start of the treatment that this process is part of the session and that the treatment does not complete until after the integration period.

In my personal practice, I find that it is during the stillness of this integration period that insight and clarity appear for me. I often listen to a piece of gentle music while my experience settles. This period of integration feels as valuable as the healing, meditation or journey that I have experienced, so make sure to allow ample time for it.

When the integration period is complete, let the client know the treatment is over. To detach from a client you can perform the *Kenyoku* Technique (see Reiki Techniques, page 196). You may also wish to cleanse the room with herbs or incense, open a window and go and wash your hands to detach fully. It is also recommended to fetch the client a glass of water and make sure they are grounded and back in this reality.

Useful Questions to Ask after a Reiki Drum Treatment

After a client's first drumming session it can be useful to gather feedback to learn more about what the client enjoys or might have found uncomfortable. It will also provide insight into how the treatment might have differed from or even exceeded their expectation. This can help you manage future sessions and tailor your introductions and marketing material to suit.

Even basic questions like, "Were you comfortable enough?", "How was the volume?", "What would you prefer next time?" or, "Was there a particular part of the treatment that you liked best?", help you shape a treatment and find your personal style that you can develop over time. If you find a client or friend who is particularly excited by the drum and wants to learn more then, again over time, you can work with them in a deeper way to explore elements of shamanism such as meeting spirit guides and exploring the shamanic worlds through the journey process.

Never underestimate the power of the drum and reiki. The drum is a powerful instrument for change and transformation. The sound waves physically move patterns of energy, so do not be surprised if the client experiences change. Give a client time to connect with their experiences and then share what feels significant about them with you.

You may feel that it's appropriate to always follow up your drumming sessions a few days later with an email or short message to offer support and reassurance for the client.

Shamanic Reiki Treatment Flow

Here's a reminder of the flow of a treatment.

Pre-session

- As soon as a session is booked, subtle energies will already be at work, so watch for dreams, signs, omens, synchronicities, unusual events, and ask the client to do so also.
- Ask your client to open their heart to what they are really seeking from the session. What is opening for them and what are they ready to leave behind?

- You could perform a diagnostic journey (see Chapter 8, page 181) to check in with your guides and feel the energy of the session to see what will be involved and check whether you are the right person to do this work.

Preparing for the Session

- Cleanse your space.
- Create the container.
- Connect with reiki and your guides (self-preparation).
- Make sure you are grounded and do a self-check-in: am I able to hold authority and compassion for this client?

Session (Pre-Treatment)

- Settle client in.
- Pre-treatment discussion with client as to what they are seeking – listen carefully.
- Find a clear intention.
- Explain the session and answer questions (explain shamanism and reiki, explain what to expect during the treatment, share the drum and how the treatment will complete).

During the Treatment

- Connect with reiki, your drum and guides, feel the safety of the container.
- Begin by using reiki to relax the client at first, raise vibrations of the energy field (5–10 mins).
- Do a short guided meditation (with or without the drum) if necessary to relax the client.
- Start your drumming (10–20 mins).
- Ask for guidance, allow spirit to move through you.
- Complete with more reiki (10–20 mins).
- Integration (Guidance may come here; maybe follow-up work like a ceremony, affirmation, creative project or time in nature is required).
- End the session as you would normally.

Post-Treatment and Feedback

- Disconnect from the client's energy once healing is complete.
- Make sure both you and the client are grounded. Offer the client water.
- Provide positive feedback and share any guidance received.
- Listen to your client share their experience if they wish.
- After-treatment care: what can you suggest to help the client integrate this healing? Where can you gently nudge the client to take action to increase their well-being?
- Make notes.
- Cleanse your energy and the space.
- Connect with nature.

TAKE ACTION **Reflections on Client Practice**

As you start to practise with clients and friends, reflect on the difference the drum brings into your reiki sessions so that you can develop your own style and understanding of what works in different situations. These questions may help you:

- How do you connect with your drum and reiki?
- How do you describe the drumming and the treatment process to the client?
- What works best as a way to relax the client?
- Do you like to scan with the drum, or your hands, or just go where you feel guided?
- What feels different about drumming versus classic reiki?
- What feels significant about the treatments? Are there any similarities?
- Is there anything you notice regarding the client's energy as you work with the drum?
- What issues do you find the drum is most effective for treating?

Make sure you get feedback from your clients so that you can listen to how the drumming treatments feel from their point of view. Find out what they enjoyed or didn't like so much, and how they felt afterwards.

Common Issues for Practitioners

No matter how much experience you have as an energy practitioner or therapist, when you pick up a drum or learn any other new technique, old patterns of anxiety and self-doubt can resurface and it can take a while to build up your confidence. This is very natural and the best way to move through these beginner's wobbles is to practise, practise and practise. Below are some common questions and pitfalls and how to overcome them.

- Thinking that you are doing it wrong. This stems from a lack of confidence and trust. Read over your notes and ask your teacher questions if you haven't understood how to perform a technique – but also remember that you are not the healer, reiki is. If you are following the process you have been taught and your intention is aligned with the client's healing request and is set for the highest good, then surrender and trust that the process you are holding is doing what it needs to do. Over time you will become more confident in the connection that you have with your drum and your guiding helpers.
- Questioning how softly or loudly to drum and feeling uncertain. The best way to know the answer to this is to practise and to listen to client feedback. Get to know the sounds and variations in tones that your drum can play.
- Not being sure of how close to drum to the client. It's really important to remember what a powerful tool for transformation the drum is and how its vibration can be felt right the way through the body. Always maintain a distance of at least 50 cm away from the head, ears and heart. Play more softly over these sensitive areas, and for less time if a client has not experienced the drum previously. Respond to your client's feedback and adjust accordingly.
- Feeling uncertain about how long to drum for. As a general rule, I suggest drumming for 10–20 minutes as part of an hour's session. A sample session might look like this:

  - Client Consultation: 10 minutes
  - Relaxation/reiki: 10 minutes
  - Drumming: 15–20 minutes
  - Reiki/Integration: 10–15 minutes
  - Feedback and closing: 10 minutes

- Not feeling confident enough to respond to client questions about the drum and what it does. Think in advance about what questions clients might have and prepare your answers from your own experience in your own words.
- Feeling unsure about how to respond to client experiences. Honour each experience that your clients have. Just like in a reiki treatment, our experience is individual and will be unique for each of us and different each time. Clients may share their experiences with you and expect you to decode them and propose their significance. Always give the power to the client. They know best what their experience means for them – it is their subconscious mind that presents it to them, after all. Encourage your clients to connect with their higher self and perhaps journal and reflect on what meaning it has for them rather than attempting to offer your interpretation. Clients can sometimes be frustrated by this, as they want you to be "the oracle" with the answers, rather than opening to and listening to the answers that they already hold within. However, one of the principal benefits of working with the drum is that it assists us in opening our intuition and connecting to the all-knowing parts of ourselves, so encourage clients to lean into this and claim their inner wisdom. If you like to work with oracle decks, it can help to offer your client the opportunity to pull a card that will help them make sense of their experience. This is a way to bridge their conscious mind of logic and reason with their imagination and sense of wonder. It also keeps the power with the client and their thoughts and feelings rather than them referring to you and yours. Invite clients to consult their own inner oracle by asking them questions about how they are feeling and what feels significant.
- Feeling unsure about what feedback and insights to share with a client. As a reiki practitioner you may be extremely sensitive to energy and deeply intuitive, or guided by helping spirits who show you information. It can feel difficult to know what to share with a client, especially when they are looking at you so expectantly. There are a few ways that I handle this. Firstly, as part of my intention at the beginning, I ask that the client receives any guidance or information in the way that they will best receive and understand it. This might mean, for example, that they receive a message, a feeling or a memory, or sense a late family member close to them, or indeed

it may mean that I receive guidance in order to share it with them because they might doubt their own intuition. Alternatively, this intention also offers a possibility that they could receive guidance from another source, such as an oracle card, for example, or a dream later that day or a chance meeting with a friend. Remember, it is not our role as reiki practitioners to diagnose, so even if you are shown information about your client's health, rather than diagnose any conditions, ask questions. For example, you may ask: Have you ever had an injury to your left knee? Have you ever had any issues with your digestion? If a client is surprised by your questions you can say that you sensed the energy felt different in those areas. If you feel there is an urgency, encourage the client to seek medical attention. Refer clients to other practitioners who can help them with specific ailments, nutritional advice, counselling or physical therapies. Some clients ask many questions about what their energy felt like and want to know what you "picked up" or sensed from the treatment. It's like they are probing for information. This is healthy curiosity; however, it's not reiki. If clients are seeking guidance for life questions or specific issues, invite them for a reading, if that is something you feel confident offering, or refer them to another practitioner who offers this. Whatever you wish to share with your client, make sure it is useful, relevant and helpful for them. Sharing for example that you saw the client in a former life as a princess in Egypt sounds magical, but in what way is that information empowering for your client today? Once during a treatment I was shown a vision of a client enslaved in a past life. Rather than share this with the client, I told them that I had a sense of entrapment, like they felt unable to escape from a situation. As it turned out, the client admitted that they were unhappy in their job; they had a new boss who they didn't get on with and felt trapped there. After the client had revealed this, I was able to gently nudge them to take baby steps towards changing this situation, we worked on healing their confidence issues and over time they were more able to stand up for themselves. Their work situation improved and they didn't even have to find a new job. Revealing information and wisdom that you receive during a treatment in a useful and positive way can help clients and be the nudge that they need. This is an art and takes practice; you will find that with some clients you feel comfortable sharing information and with others not so much. If in doubt, ask to be guided and know that when reiki is flowing, you are working for a client's highest good.

- Feeling worried about disturbing neighbours, both residential and businesses. Guess what? The drum makes noise and some folks just don't like it, they don't get it, they don't want to hear about it and they certainly do not want it interfering with their day or even the peaceful evening watching TV that they had planned. Be prepared for this and find a suitable location where you can drum to your heart's content. If you rent a room in a salon or therapy centre, double-check that everyone there is in agreement with your using it for drumming and does not mind the sound. Over the years I have been extremely lucky with neighbours and fellow therapists alike. I used to run a monthly reiki drum healing circle in Edinburgh and in the neighbouring room, separated by a very thin joining wall, was a therapist running counselling sessions at the same time. It was fortuitous that she and her clients gladly welcomed the drum and incorporated the repetitive beats into their sessions. Not everyone reacts in this way, so do your research before you set yourself up, to avoid disappointment and niggles from neighbours.

TAKE ACTION   **Release and Restore with Earth Energy**

Here we work with the bubbling spring point on the soles of the feet and the energetic circuit that naturally invites nourishment from the Earth to flow into the body. I shared this in Chapter 2. It is a wonderful way to help clients relax and open to the nourishing and revitalizing energy of the Earth. I recommend doing this outside in nature if possible, and suggest that as well as offering this to clients and friends, you do it for yourself whenever you can while self-treating with reiki.

Invite your client to lie down and get comfortable on the Earth, on a yoga mat or directly on the grass if they are happy with that. Direct them to bend their legs and keep them hip-width apart or at a distance that is comfortable. Make sure the soles of their feet are in connection with the Earth. Rather than place a cushion under their head, which may be too bulky, I suggest a paperback book or two. This ensures the neck is not overly extended and is in alignment with the natural curves of the spine; it will also help with keeping the energy points at the top of the spine open so that energy can flow. Ask them to place their arms by their sides with palms facing up, which will open the shoulders and also help them open to the *chi* of the heavens while they are supported by the Earth.

Prepare yourself in your usual way, inviting in guides and reiki to support and guide you. Also acknowledge the place in nature where you are and any other nature beings or plants that you sense are present.

Invite the client to close their eyes, relax and take long, slow, deep breaths into their belly. Begin to drum very softly and very slowly.

Invite them to visualize golden roots anchoring them into the Earth, holding them lovingly, reaching down into the centre of the Earth.

With the drumbeat slow and steady, talk them through a body scan, inviting them to relax and release tension from the body. Start at the feet and work your way up to the head. Suggest that they visualize this tension releasing from the back of their body into the Earth, where it can be composted. If it feels like there is a lot of releasing, then you may notice your drumbeat shifting too.

Bring their awareness to the bubbling spring, activating the receiving channels, and invite them to imagine receiving a golden, nourishing nectar of revitalizing energy into their body. You may like to use the reiki symbols here to assist with this connection, emotional release, or to bring extra focus to the treatment. As you focus on the receiving aspect you may notice that your drumbeat changes and you feel guided to move around, up and down the client's body. Allow yourself to be guided, of course.

Next, bring their awareness to the palms of their hands, which are facing upwards into the sky. Suggest that they visualize the palms being filled with light; shift your drumbeat accordingly. Then invite them to place their hands on an area of their body to receive this healing light into their being.

If there are plants present, such as a tree, you may find that they also want to help with the healing. If it feels right to do so then open to this accordingly.

To complete you may wish to lay down your drum and sit quietly next to your client, beaming reiki at them for five minutes or so. It may be perfect to allow the sounds of nature to infuse the treatment, or, if you are in a more urban and noisy environment, play a soothing track that will keep the client in a relaxed state. Give thanks to your helpers, the space and your drum when you have finished, and bring the client back to this reality slowly. They may need time to come round and help getting up. Ensure you are both grounded before you shift gears into this reality.

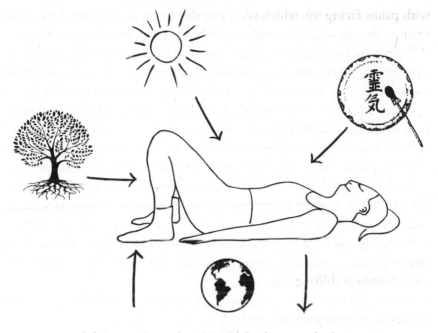

Release, receive, and restore with Earth energy, the drum,
reiki, nature, and heavenly energy.

Helping Clients Make Positive Change

The drum is a catalyst for change. You can feel that power in just one simple beat. The sound waves get things moving in mind, body and spirit and help shift imbalances. As a reiki professional, that's what you are holding space for. You are holding a clear loving space that helps your clients shine a light on those areas of their health and well-being that need attention, that need love, that need to come back into balance, that need to change. You will know from your experience that there are many layers to our healing path and restoring our true nature. It's not unusual for clients to begin a series of treatments with a certain intention, only to find that it has benefited other areas in their life that they hadn't realized needed attention, but that they feel so much better now they have been transformed. In the previous chapter I shared how you can work with the drum to create a new story for yourself with affirmations, visualization and intention. The same is true for working with clients in your practice. As well as working on your personal vision, you can help clients to create a new and positive story. In the reiki drum technique this is taught as mindset reprogramming. If you have a client who is eager to combat addiction, bad habits or is willing to change their negative self-talk, for example, you might want to experiment with this technique. The process connects to the subconscious with reiki and focuses the mind on something positive to manifest. The drum and reiki travel to the cause of where this negative pattern took root and help to remove it. It can be more beneficial to work on this technique over a series of treatments, such as three treatments spaced 2–4 weeks apart, rather than one single treatment, so that yourself and the client can see progress and note shifts that occur. Be sure to get feedback from your client so that you can listen to how this treatment felt from their point of view. Find out what they enjoyed or didn't like so much, what they found useful and how they felt afterwards.

Personally speaking, it has not been a treatment area that I have been guided to flow with in my professional practice, so I tend to work with it for my own personal healing rather than with clients.

When the Client Wants to Drum

If you have several drums and feel guided to offer a client the opportunity to drum, this can make for a really interesting and expansive healing session. Some clients will feel very drawn to the drum (just like us) and so handing them a drum can be like offering them the opportunity to reclaim their power over their health and well-being: mental, emotional, physical and spiritual. Sessions like this can work well if the client feels like they are carrying a lot of tension or anxiety that need to be released, are feeling blocked or at an impasse in their life, feel disconnected, depressed, alone or lost or feel like they have pent-up emotions or anger that they need to express. I would generally offer a session like this to a client who has already experienced several in-person sessions with reiki and the drum. There are many ways to facilitate this, so here are some guidelines to follow when you are in the session.

Clarify the client's intention to begin.

Get them acquainted with the drum and how it sounds. Let them hold the drum close to them and speak (silently) their intentions into the drum. The client can send reiki to the drum by placing their hands on the drum head, if they are attuned to it.

Reassure the client that there is no wrong way to drum and that they don't need to be musically trained or perceive themselves as a musical person in order to play.

Begin to play your drum with the support of reiki (and the symbols), with the intention to hold the space and facilitate this healing for the client. I find it easier to be standing so that you can both freely express the movement and rhythm that wants to come through. If your client cannot or does not want to stand, then seated will work fine.

You may wish to gently drum over the client's energy field and encourage them to begin to drum when they feel ready.

You might find the client drums very softly at first. This is quite normal, so be supportive and encouraging. Remind the client of their intention to keep them focused. Allow them to explore.

After about fifteen minutes, bring the drumming to a close and ask the client to put down their drum and sit or lie down. Place your hands on the client or simply beam reiki to them for the remainder of your session or however long you feel is required. Play music to help them land and integrate the experience.

Close as you would close a reiki session and listen closely to your client's feedback, asking them what they experienced during the drumming and how they feel now.

Taking a Client on a Journey with the Reiki Drum

When you feel confident with the shamanic reiki journey technique that I outlined in Chapter 3 and have been journeying for a period of time that has enabled you to explore the shamanic realms and created a strong relationship with a guide, you may feel ready to hold space for a client to journey.

This is something to work up to as I feel that it's not until you are confident in the journey space yourself that you can instruct others to do so. If it doesn't appeal to you then doing this for others may not be for you. I'm sure you will be guided as to what feels right.

Similarly, it may take some time for clients to understand and become interested in the different aspects of healing and self-exploration that the drum offers as part of the shamanic reiki journey. When the time is right, clients will step forwards with enthusiasm and a wish to know more about shamanic practice, wanting to explore the shamanic worlds and connect with spirit guides. This is your cue: if you feel confident, introduce them to the shaman's journey.

As time goes by and you find yourself accumulating more instruments and drums, you may feel guided to hold healing sessions while the client drums with you and embodies the practice for themself. For my part, my practice with the drum and journey healing developed more with groups rather than individuals, and this might also be the case for you. You can read more about this in Chapter 8, page 155 which is dedicated to drumming circles.

~

Here are some guidelines for client journey work:
- Prepare yourself and your space and invite in your guides, helpers and reiki.
- Charge up yourself and your drum with reiki.
- Describe the journey process and experience to the client. Tell them what to expect. Use your own words and examples from your own experience.
- Invite them to create an affirmation and also an intention for the journey. Keep this simple, such as: *"Journey to meet a guide to show me the shamanic worlds"* or *"Journey to meet an animal spirit to bring back my power."*
- Make sure they have a clear idea of their access point. This could be a place in nature that they can visualize themselves being in from which to start the journey.
- Explain the different steps of the process and demonstrate the drum rhythm.
- When you are both ready, invite the client to lie on the treatment couch. Cover them if needed, and you may like to provide a blindfold or scarf to cover their eyes so that they can focus their attention inwards without distractions.
- You may like to lead them through a short meditation and a short hands-on reiki session (10 minutes) before you begin, so that they are more relaxed and open.
- Carry out the shamanic reiki drum journey using the structure that makes sense to you. Change the rhythm to break up the different parts of the process and use different symbols as you are guided. This makes it easy for the client to relax and navigate.
- When the drumming is complete, make sure the client is fully back in this reality. Work with the power symbol to ground them.
- Play music for 5–10 minutes and carry out hands-on reiki or beam reiki to the client while they integrate this experience.

- Finish your treatment, thank your guides and disconnect from the client's energy field as you would following a regular reiki session.
- Let the client know that the experience is complete and offer them paper if necessary so they can make notes. Allow them to be with their experience rather than rushing to tell it to you.
- Offer the client water to help them ground and come back round to this reality.
- Ask the client how they are feeling now. Listen to what they have to say and provide feedback. Ask questions about their experience, what feels significant and how they feel about it. The feeling and the frequency is KEY. Remember the journey is a metaphor.
- Reassure the client that they have done everything perfectly. Often they may doubt themselves and think it's all in their imagination. If the client says that nothing really happened, then be sure to ask them to elaborate and listen to how they are feeling. Do not attempt to find meaning in a client's experience; rather, ask them what significance they think it has.
- Make sure you are able to frame any guidance that you have received on the client's behalf in a positive way.
- Close the space and disconnect from the client's energy field as you normally do.
- Follow up with your client in a few days to see how they are doing. If they received guidance and was asked to take action in some way, then gently nudge them to honour what came through.

Distance Healing with Reiki and the Drum

If you are familiar with giving distance reiki treatments and are trained to reiki Level 2 then you will already have been taught and have experience of giving reiki over a distance to clients or friends and family who are not physically present with you. It is very easy to incorporate the use of the drum into distance healing sessions and, with the addition of modern technology, the options for delivery are better than ever.

What Are the Options for Distance Drumming Treatments?

- Meet online at an agreed time for a live treatment, using a live service such as Zoom, Skype or FaceTime.

- Meet online or over the phone before and after the treatment and work with your drum and reiki remotely. At an agreed time, your client will lie down in a quiet space to "receive" the healing that you are remotely sending with reiki and the drum.
- Record the reiki drum session and send it to the client to listen to at a time that suits them.

Advantages of Live Online Treatments

- Create rapport and empathy with a client when you meet online at a specified time and chat about the treatment and their intention.
- Instantly receive feedback from the client during or at the end of the session.
- Can be carried out at times that suit you both, regardless of physical distance, health or access issues.

Disadvantages of Live Online Treatments

- The success of the delivery is highly dependent on the internet connection and technological ability of both yourself and the client – this can be a huge distraction.
- The drumbeat will often not transfer very effectively over the internet and the sound levels or quality can get distorted – again, this is a huge distraction.
- You may feel limited by what you wish to do because of the screen.
- The client can get distracted by things happening their end like visitors to the house, pets and other family members. You cannot control their environment.
- It's harder to control the sacred space.
- It can be hard to keep yourself energized and focused, or gain rapport with the client, because there is no client physically in your space.

Here are a few pointers to help you when you are working with your drum over a distance, whatever method you choose.

- Always prepare yourself and your space in the same way that you would if the client was present with you. Power up your drum before beginning, either by drawing each symbol over the drum or simply by holding the drum in your hands with reiki flowing.

- Surround yourself with objects in your space that support you and fill you with energy.
- Make sure your client completes a client record sheet in advance of the session and is clear on their intention for the healing.
- Make sure that you have fully explained the process so that the client understands what will happen and what they need to do. If your treatment is live, reassure the client that should either of you lose connection during the session, rather than interrupt the treatment attempting to reconnect, you will simply carry on and they will still feel the benefits.
- Always be mindful of what you are doing and stay present. Do not attach yourself to the outcome but simply let reiki, your guides and your drum do their thing and let all healing be done for the highest good.
- When you have finished, detached and grounded, reconnect with the client to provide feedback and aftercare advice. If the client falls asleep and doesn't respond, suggest they contact you later.

Guidelines for a Remote Drumming Treatment

- Set up your treatment couch as usual and set an intention that your client is present. You could also place a teddy bear or pillow in their place to represent your client.
- Start the treatment by sending distance reiki to relax the client. Use the Level 2 symbols in the way that you have been taught. There are many techniques for this such as using a photo, placing your hands on yourself or a teddy bear that represents the client, or beaming reiki at the computer screen if the client is online live with you. I often like to use my drum to represent the client; I place my hands on the drum head with the intention that the client be filled with reiki.
- If your client is online live with you, you may like to talk them through a guided visualization or meditation.
- Drum as if the client was present, moving over the body (teddy bear) or around the treatment couch, working with different drumbeats and symbols as guided for 10–15 minutes.
- Complete the treatment with a further session of reiki using your preferred distance reiki method. If you are using a teddy bear then you can simply place your hands on it; I often do this.

- End the treatment in your usual way. Make sure you give thanks to your drum, to reiki and to all the helping spirits. You can close the session with a large power symbol; and make sure you detach from the client's energy field.
- You may like to play a piece of relaxing music to allow the client time to adjust, integrate and come back to meet you onscreen.
- Provide feedback for the client if they are present live, or write notes to email or call them with afterwards.
- After the treatment, cleanse the space and your teddy (if using) and drum. Make sure you disconnect fully from the client's energy field and are grounded.

Distance Healing with the Shamanic Drumming Journey

In Chapter 4, I introduced the idea of experiencing reiki as part of the shamanic journey. The "Take Action" exercise in that chapter was to give yourself healing; however, the same process can be followed to offer healing to a client in the shamanic realms.

You can choose to drum or, alternatively, listen to a drumming track to help you enter the journey state. In your journey your intention will be to send reiki for the highest good to the client as per their intention. It can also be a good opportunity to ask for information on behalf of the client that will help them with their healing process. Pay attention during the journey, as everything that you experience and are shown will be part of the healing process for the client and will have specific meaning. Make sure you make thorough notes. Unless you are well acquainted with your guides, you may not fully understand what they are showing you. This technique takes practice, though it is a very informative way to offer healing remotely.

Since this technique does not require the presence of the client, if I undertake this type of healing journey I will do so remotely at an agreed time rather than via an online link and then provide feedback to the client at an agreed time or via email.

Distance Drumming Healing for Multiple Clients

When multiple people request healing, it can be simpler to send one group healing that includes everyone. Write each name on a piece of paper, include as much detail as you have (such as names, ages, location, what healing needs to be given) and make sure you have their permission. After you have completed your list, empower the page and your drum with the reiki symbols and intend that they be filled with reiki, or simply hold the paper over your drum in your hands. Visualize the people receiving the treatment and pick up and play your drum. Try this for about twenty minutes. Work as you feel guided. Use a teddy bear (or several) to drum over if you prefer that method.

Programming Distant Treatments

If you intend to send distance healing to a client on a regular basis, i.e., daily for a week, it may be useful to programme the healing for the whole week and programme it to send on consecutive days rather than sending the healing every day. State, as part of your intention when sending the distant treatment, the time that the client will receive the healing from reiki and your drum. Try this and listen to any feedback the recipient has.

Sending Reiki to Future Events

Using the technique above, you can also intend that reiki be sent at a certain time for someone in the future. This may be necessary if someone is scheduled to undergo an operation or has an important event for which they may require healing, or needs emotional/mental support for something like a business meeting or job interview.

Drumming Reiki to a Global Situation

Send the high vibration of loving light for the positive outcome of a global situation. You may wish to release fear, and visualize kindness and peace to all. Set the intention for this loving energy to continue until all is resolved. Adapt to the global situation occurring. You may wish to invite other reiki practitioners to join you to amplify the effect.

Why Bother Drumming Reiki When Recipients Can't Hear the Drumbeat?

You may indeed be wondering what is the point in working with the drum and reiki over a distance when the recipient cannot physically feel the drum or experience the sound. Fair question! In my experience, working with the drum adds a whole new level of intensity to the reiki treatment. The drum is a powerful tool, especially when used in conjunction with your intention to heal. This has an effect regardless of proximity. I invite you to practise for yourself. You may find that the act of drumming helps you to stay focused more easily than simply sending reiki. Experiment with clients by sending distance reiki in your regular way and then add in the drum. Ask clients what they notice is different and reflect on what is different for you as the practitioner. If you don't find this effective or enjoyable, then you may find it more satisfactory to record personal mini drum healings for clients, uniquely recorded at the time of sending the healing, with the intention that whenever the client listens to the track, they will receive the healing that they require. Again, client feedback and guidance from your drum and your helpers will lead you in the direction that your reiki drum practice is meant to go.

Shamanic Reiki Ethics

The professional ethics and code of conduct for a shamanic reiki practitioner working with the drum or other tools follow the same guidelines as those of a reiki practitioner.

The practice of reiki teaches you to obtain permission from the recipient before beginning a treatment and to explain the process thoroughly so that the recipient understands what is involved. Always make sure that your intention is to send reiki for the highest good.

Never offer reiki and then switch to shamanic reiki with the drum without explanation or consent. Be clear about what treatment you are offering and what that treatment involves.

Be sensitive to a client's energy field and always keep the drum a minimum distance of 15 cm above the body, maintaining a distance of 30–50 cm away from their head, throat, and ears. Stop the drumming if your client is uncomfortable. Make sure they feel safe.

Never journey to find guidance or offer healing on a client's behalf if they have not given you permission to do so; this is highly intrusive.

I was taught never to send reiki to someone whose permission I do not have. Under normal circumstances I always like to chat to clients who have requested the healing and get clear on their intentions. Often clients may request healing for friends and family and, in these cases, ideally you want to know that those people are open to receiving healing and that you do have their permission. Sometimes, for example if you are sending reiki to a global situation, you may not personally receive permission from the individuals affected because you simply do not know them. In cases like this, when I send reiki I ask that it will flow to those who are open to receive it, and if they are not open to receive healing then I invite it to either flow into the Earth to be transformed by the Earth, or for the reiki to be held in space and time for when that person may be open to receiving. If this doesn't appeal to you then don't offer reiki in this way. Alternatively, you may already be well versed in sending distance healing and have a method that you feel comfortable working with.

Remember when treating pregnant women to ask permission from the baby in the womb before starting the treatment. I personally do not like to treat women who are in the first trimester of pregnancy because I know that this can be a very sensitive time and risk of miscarriage is high.

Never proceed if you do not feel comfortable, if you don't have the energy to hold space or if you cannot feel compassion for the client. DO NOT proceed if the client is under the influence of drugs or alcohol.

Remember you are not the healer, you are the conduit for the healing, like a hollow bone for the healing energy to flow through. This can only happen if the person/being you are treating is ready to heal and willing to let themselves heal.

The UK Reiki Federation has a useful code of ethics on their website that it's worth taking a look at.

Shamanic Reiki Cautions and Contraindications

As with traditional reiki, each client should be assessed on their individual needs and situation. Reiki, as you will have been taught, cannot cause harm and is taken by the client as needed. Please be aware, however, of the following when working with your drum or other sound instruments:

- Working with the drum is not recommended for epileptic clients.
- Caution is required for clients with a history of severe emotional disorders, schizophrenia, psychosis or hallucination problems. The drum often induces imagery and it is imperative that the individual be able to distinguish what is real in ordinary reality. If in doubt, medical/psychological advice should be sought where appropriate.
- Caution is required for clients with pacemakers, stents or shunts. Do not use the drum directly on or above a pacemaker or defibrillator. Keep a distance of at least 30 cm from where it is implanted.

- Exercise caution with women in the first trimester of pregnancy as this is a very sensitive time. Traditional sound therapy advises against treating women in the first trimester. Remember that the foetus is highly sensitive to sound. Use your own judgement and do what you feel comfortable with. As I explained earlier, I personally do not treat clients in this first trimester.

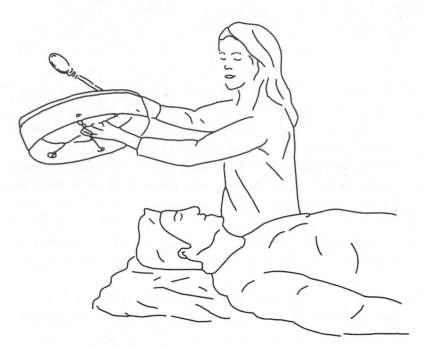

Drum at least 50 cm away from the head.

The Drum in the Reiki Share

A reiki share is an opportunity for students, teachers and professionals of all levels and lineages of reiki to get together to exchange and share reiki.

In my experience, reiki shares are fundamental not only for providing continued support in your reiki practice but also for offering that essential pillar of self-care, so needed and often overlooked by those in the healing arena.

Reiki shares also act as an informal space to ask questions and discuss reiki experiences and techniques among your peers. Often in these reiki shares there may also be an element of distance healing to loved ones or areas of the world and situations that the group feels guided to send healing to. When we gather and join our intentions to heal, the healing frequency is magnified. A reiki share can also be a wonderful environment into which to introduce your drum and practise among supportive friends and friendly faces.

Seven Ways to Share Your Drum in a Reiki Share

1. Introduce the group to the drum with a short meditation at the beginning of your session together. This will relax the whole group and give them a short taster of the drum.
2. Offer a guided reiki drumming journey experience to the whole group. Start with a simple twenty-minute journey and explain the process step by step. A simple journey to start with would be one with an intention like "to connect with the source of reiki". Invite participants to self-treat with reiki at the same time. You can complete this by beaming reiki to the group to help them integrate the journey experience.
3. If the group has experienced the drum before, you may wish to offer a more specific journey, such as intention to meet a guide and find out about some information. If there is time, you can lead the group in a sharing around their experiences
4. Share your drum with individuals by offering to drum over a participant instead of offering them hands-on reiki as part of the reiki share.
5. Offer a group reiki drumming healing in which the whole group is lying down to receive healing at the same time. This time you will walk around the whole group and drum over each participant in turn.
6. Instead of classic distance reiki healing, while the rest of the group is sending distance reiki together you can beat your drum and use it to send distance reiki with the same intention.
7. If the group shares a mutual feeling, goal or desire, you can use your drum to bring momentum to these. Create a shared affirmation and follow the process outlined in Chapter 4. Finding and working towards common goals in this way can strengthen group bonds, increase feelings of connection and bring groups of reiki practitioners together.

Drumming and Reiki in the Workplace

For several years I was a closet reiki practitioner, offering client treatments on Fridays and weekends while smiling my way through an office-based 9-to-5 role the rest of the week. After picking up the drum, my practice gained a new momentum and the drum helped me to bridge the gap between "reiki Fay" and "office Fay". I organized a lunchtime meditation group and, amazingly, a room that I had never even previously known about appeared for us to use. Little did they know that I was bringing the drum with me (and the silent power of reiki). Before long, a small group of my office colleagues were joining me to relax to the meditative beat of the drum accompanied by the supportive flow of reiki energy.

If you are finding it hard to combine working with your healing gifts and working in a different job – like I – did then offering relaxation and meditation (with your drum and reiki) to colleagues as part of employee well-being may also be a way forward for you. You can read more about holding drum circles in Chapter 7, page 155.

The lunchtime group certainly opened doors for me. Not in terms of moving through the corporate world with my practice, but its gift was valuable experience and confidence that propelled me forwards.

TAKE A BEAT

As shown in this chapter, there are a variety of ways to introduce the drum into your reiki sessions. As you invite the rhythm of the drum into your healing space, your clients, your drum and your spirit team will all show you the path. Different techniques, maybe even more shamanic tools or instruments, will make themselves known to you and your own unique style of reiki drum and shamanic practice will develop. The power, as always, is in your intention. The more you drum, the more you will feel connected to something so much greater than you. The next chapter takes you on a journey though ceremony, celebration and healing to connect you in a deeper way to the spirit of all things. Honouring the Earth, the natural cycles, moon and stars, I will share practices to help you become a clearer bridge between heaven and Earth.

6

Connecting Heaven and Earth

Of all the myriad ways that playing the drum helps us to heal and realign with our truth, by far the most informative, exciting and expansive way, and the one that most speaks to my heart, is playing the drum outside with the natural world. With nature as my backdrop, my witness and receiver of the reiki and the drum rhythm that flows, I feel a deep sense of peace, connection and unity. Whether as an instrument for healing ourselves, others, plants, waterways or places in the landscape or as a tool for connection, that enables us to merge and feel the pulse of the living world, the drum opens unseen doorways and accelerates us through them to remind us that we are nature.

Simply drumming for joy at the water's edge, in the forest, in your back garden, to the moon, under a downpour, or by a lonesome pine is a way to show gratitude to the natural world around you. This token of acknowledgement and thanks is felt as a ripple throughout the universe and brings you into alignment with your very own dance and healing process. It reminds you that we are all connected and you are not alone; you are part of a much greater and powerful whole. This will shift your frequency and that of the world around you, helping to bring about harmony and wholeness.

In my previous books, *Plant Spirit Reiki* and *Plants That Speak, Souls That Sing,* I have spoken at length about the destructive division and illusion of separateness that we have placed between us and the natural world: a cause of both mental and physical illness throughout the world and one we are only now starting to take seriously. Both reiki and the drum help to weave together again those parts of us that feel separate from ourselves, each other and the wilder world. Connecting in this way can help to engender a sense of rootedness, a feeling of strength and support and a sense of belonging that leads to communities that care, not just about their own livelihoods and health, but also about those of the planet. This is the heaven on Earth that we in our hearts are all here to bring into creation now.

A Creation Story

From a journey with a plant spirit reiki, 19 July 2021

Energy roars through me like a golden light beam, like a tap that cannot turn off.

It's out of the box, it's out of the bag, the light cannot be dimmed, it cannot be caught and held under cover.

The light is out and reaching far and wide.

It will never go back.

I try to close my mouth but it contains the stars.

My eyes open as wide as the sun with golden pools of light pooling, widening like sinkholes.

I tilt my head back and try to roar but a muffled golden sound rings out like koshi bells.

This is not the god of thunder, rain or war. This is the goddess of light.

As if this great light that pierces my being strips me of all physical form, my body falls away.

Now it really is too bright and blinding to see.

What really is me?

Where do I begin or end?

That which is not me is so bright with my light that it seems like me and as soon as I make that realization, we merge and fuse together as one – now larger and brighter than before.

And that's how it starts.

Shining brightly, working your light.

It seems so innocent at first but as the form drops and your light attracts more light, you become larger than you ever dreamt possible.

Your energy is all-encompassing.

You become me, we become each other.

This is the way love grows, I think.

This is why we shine, I believe.

Those that weren't shining when you began, sure are now.

Their light nurtures you, like a beacon in a storm.

There is so much light and expansion it feels like it will go on for ever and then something else happens.

Like an elastic that was forever stretching and threatening to break,

You don't break
You
We
Implode.
The universe takes a huge, deep in-breath and we are sucked
through the mouth of the great god into the void.
Here we breathe and we begin again.
We begin to remember what it is to shine.

Drumming with Nature

If you are familiar with the symbols that are taught at reiki Level 2, you will be used to the distance symbol, also called the connection symbol. The energy of this symbol reminds us that we are one; it transcends time and space, merging all moments into one. This enables us to send healing to what we perceive to be the past or into the future and to others who are not physically with us. For me, the drum carries a similar ability to connect us to all and everything, helping us to drop our form and merge with the consciousness of the universe. With this in mind, we can embark on a curious adventure, getting to experience and feel the pulse of the natural world. I like to use the distance/connection symbol whenever I drum with nature too, to facilitate the connection. If you are not familiar with the symbol then you will simply drum with a clear intention. As always when I drum, I will call forwards my helping team of spirit guides to be with me for protection and guidance, and I suggest you do the same to help you feel supported and safe.

Extract from a Journey to discover what the Consciousness of the Earth has to say

I am sleeping or so you think
My constant fires of creation go unnoticed in the hearts of
*   many*
How do you think that makes me feel?
Unnoticed, taken for granted, abandoned.
Do not abandon me.
For I do not leave you.
Mother of all things I keep creating

Mother of all things I lie waiting
Mother of all things I deeply sigh inside
Mother of all things you will not see me cry
For Mother I am and mother I do
Loving all my children as they dance
You are nothing without me
And yet, I am everything with you
We are one, together we-earth.

TAKE ACTION Drum to Connect with the Heartbeat of the Earth

Outside in nature, hold in your heart the intention to connect with the heartbeat of the Earth, the pulse of nature, and then allow yourself to be guided with reiki flowing. Feel the Earth beneath your feet. Open yourself to the heartbeat of the Earth. Notice how your rhythm feels and shifts and where you sense it in your body. What feelings does it bring up for you? Enjoy this experience and notice how you feel afterwards. You could also experience this lying down with a friend drumming.

Connect with and Honour the Land Where You Live

This is often overlooked by those practising healing modalities, but is helpful for creating safe spaces that are held with light and clear intention. Whether you are in a city or out in the countryside, the landscape is holding you as you make a cup of tea, send an email or give reiki to a client. Many of us spend time and money decorating our homes and treatment spaces with items that inspire joy or carry an uplifting frequency; however, we may also often neglect to honour the land that is holding us. So let's acknowledge that! If this is new to you then I suggest first starting with the intention to connect with the land where you live. As with the previous ideas, invite in your guides and reiki to flow as you drum. Drum your gratitude and your joy for all the land provides for you. After you have drummed enough, spend time in silence. You may feel guided to beam reiki out into the space around you, chant or sing a song, and during this quiet time you may also receive information from the land.

When we ran the flower farm in Nova Scotia, each season I would drum around the fields acknowledging the land, whispering my wishes, sharing my heart, and listening for what was needed. At the end of the season, when the frost had put an end to the flowering plants for that year and it was time to put the farm to bed for the winter, I would drum again. This time my intention was full of gratitude, reverence, respect, and love for the plants that had so beautifully provided for us during the past summer.

As you become more familiar with drumming and sending reiki in this way, you may repeat this with different intentions that are more specific to your home space, reiki space, work space, and so on. I also suggest connecting with the space of any event that you might be organizing or place you may be travelling to, on holiday for example, by journeying to meet the spirit of the place. You will find that this helps create a deeper sense of harmony for the spaces in which you live and work. Having made a connection through exercises like this, it is therefore imperative to maintain the connection and continue to honour and acknowledge the spirit of the land or the space, either as you create sacred space for your work or in your personal practice or as you go about your life with offerings of prayer and reiki. Drumming to call in protection to a property or area of the landscape can feel necessary if there is a threat from the outside world such as a neighbourhood dispute, people using the land to illegally dump, or if an area high in wildlife is threatened by urban development or pollution. In these cases, if you are able to access the property I recommend walking the boundaries with your drum. I like to use the power symbol in conjunction with the drum as well as inviting in the helping spirits. If you are not able to access a property, then send distance reiki, either with or without your drum.

The Spirit of Argentina

Example journey to the spirit of a place before travelling

Intention to journey to the spirit of Argentina, to be shown what I need to know for my trip.

With my unicorn guide I was taken to a large white statue of a bird/angel that felt like a familiar feeling. This transformed into a ray of diamond light, it was very magical and I stepped into the light. To my surprised I received HEALING (underlined three times in my journal!). I felt this all over my body with a message of opening, allowing, accepting, welcoming and sharing.

I took this as a good sign for the trip I had ahead of me and that it was all I needed to know at the time.

Meet and Bless the Spirits of Nature, the Trees, Plants, and Flowers

There may be an aspect of the natural world that is calling you, or you might simply feel guided to honour the beauty of your local park or your own garden and show your gratitude to the nature beings by drumming and celebrating with joy.

TAKE ACTION Drum to Meet and Bless the Spirits of Nature

As we have done previously, drum and be open to the experience. If you don't know where to start then take yourself to a place in nature, invite reiki to flow and have your guides with you. Begin to drum as you take yourself for a walk. Each drumbeat is a blessing to nature. Notice where you feel guided to go and allow your drum rhythm to flow. You may feel drawn to specific areas or plants.

Enjoy the adventure and allow yourself time to be in the frequency of the place or plant that is calling to you. Allow yourself to use your voice, make sounds and sing. Allow yourself to receive a message. This may be in the form of a colour, a feeling, a sensation, a memory, a shape, an image or even a word. You may find that it is worth a repeat visit and has a quest for you, so be prepared!

Trees as Space Holders

Over the first lockdown in 2020 my reiki practice took on a new dimension with a group of trees in my garden. Together with a group of four other reiki practitioners, I set up a distance healing circle to help soothe anxiety and bring a sense of peace for those who requested it. We each agreed to anchor our individual practices with a tree in nature so that the strength and power of the Earth and trees could hold this powerful healing.

The trees in my garden that called to me to participate were a grove of eucalyptus. Each day I visited the trees to create sacred space, tune in and send distance reiki both with and without the drum as part of the group's intention. As the days passed, I began to feel an increased sense of connection to the trees and a strong sense of feeling held and witnessed. After completing the distance healing, I lingered more in the space, giving space for my feelings, needs and desires. Some days I felt that simply by showing up and acknowledging the trees, sitting with a cup of tea in the stillness, I was receiving a transmission of healing and connection. It felt as if the trees were holding me automatically, together with the group, without me even needing to ask.

I have always felt nature to be powerful, vibrant and supportive, but this experience over the summer months opened a new doorway of appreciation and connection for me. While our distance reiki healing project has morphed into something else, my connection with these trees still remains. This grove of eucalyptus has become a power spot in my garden, with a palpable sense of vibrancy and magic. It has become a place in which I hold ceremony, send reiki with and without the drum and self-treat with reiki. I also hold healing sessions with clients over an online link from within the grove so that they too can feel held and supported by the trees and nature beings that call this space home.

TAKE ACTION Meeting a Tree with Your Drum

Outside, find a tree that you sense might be willing to connect with you and might enjoy your drum and reiki. This may be a tree that you already know well and have shared reiki with, or it may be a new friend who you feel is calling your attention. Spend as long as you need to in the presence of the tree, observing how it grows, admiring its beauty and sensing its energy. You may feel guided also to touch the tree and send reiki, or simply breathe with it. Call in guides to help you and invite reiki to flow if you haven't already. Drum with the intention to meet the spirit of the tree and ask if it will support you in your practice.

If the space allows, lean, either standing or seated, with your back against the tree so that you are physically connected as you drum. You may like to have your eyes closed and see yourself dive through the roots or climb up the branches in your inner vision. Or you may prefer to keep your eyes open and simply feel the vibration through your body and receive with all of your senses. You may be guided to move about and dance, or stay rooted like the tree. If the connection with the tree feels positive then invite it to show you its power and wisdom. Ask it how you can support each other.

Drum until you feel complete; you may then feel guided to send reiki to the tree and this will also help you to physically calm yourself after the drumming. Give thanks to the tree, to reiki and other supporting guides as you close the session. Stay in the company of the tree while you ground yourself and come back to this reality. Have your notebook handy (or phone) to record any insights that flow. Is this tree an ally for you? How can you develop your relationship further? What else is needed? Remember that you can also connect with this tree remotely when you are not together. You may feel it necessary to take a small token like a leaf, flower or seed from the tree with you to place on your altar, or take a photo of it.

Drumming with reiki to meet the spirit of a tree.

Become the Frequency of Nature

You already know through your reiki practice that everything has a vibration, a specific resonance, and in the natural world everything is communicating all of the time. Recognizing this and reflecting it back is a deep blessing and helps to build the bridge between us and the world around us. Can you feel this resonance with objects around your home, workplace or out in nature? Often a reiki practitioner might hold out their palms to sense this; others may find that they feel it elsewhere in their bodies. Experiment with your drum. Can you match the resonance of a specific flower, tree, object or place in nature? What happens when you try? It's not just the natural world that carries a resonance, but also everything in your home. Look around where you are reading this now. Perhaps you can see a chair, a cushion, a coffee mug. What happens when you pick up your drum and feel for the vibration of these objects? Can you drum to honour the journey of all of these objects and radiate their frequency back to them? Have a play and notice how the atmosphere inside shifts when you do this. Where else can you do this to increase a sense of connection and respect for all things within the web of life?

Celebrating Seasons and Cycles

Celebration in ceremony with our drums and song is a great way to show and share our appreciation of the natural world, which in turns builds those bridges and brings us closer to our natural allies. Drumming solo with joy with your favourite plant, tree, vegetable garden or in your favourite place is enough to show your gratitude. However, with a group of willing drummers it can be double the fun and can increase the frequency.

Suggestions for Group Celebration Ceremonies

- Celebrate your harvest from the garden.
- Celebrate a special time of year like solstice, equinox, birthdays, anniversaries.
- Share and celebrate your favourite plants, herbs or trees.
- Celebrate and bring healing to a landscape or a waterway.
- Celebrate and give thanks to a place that supports you.
- Create ceremony to honour a specific element like fire or water.
- Celebrate achievements, milestones, goals and phases of life.

Ceremony and Ritual

Ceremony has a place anywhere for every occasion and is a vital part of the healing process. It opens the lines of communication between us and the powers of the universe and helps deepen our relationships with the other worlds and helping spirits. You can create ceremony in your sacred space alone or for yourself and a client, or in a larger space outside with a group of like-minded souls. Group ceremony or ritual is very powerful; just think of tribal dances, or warriors chanting together. The energy that this raises, and the excitement, is a very potent force that can create change. I think of ritual as being different to ceremony. For me, ritual feels more like a regular practice that might fit into my daily routine.

An example might be a repeated way of doing something that I have developed for a certain purpose, like preparing my sacred space. Whereas ceremony carries the unique and sacred energy of a particular occasion and intention that may also involve elements of ritual. What rituals have you already created as part of your healing practice?

The Role of Ceremony and Ritual

- To honour the helping spirits or ancestors and invite in their assistance.
- To celebrate life, the seasons and cycles.
- To acknowledge rites of passage and initiation such as birth, marriage, motherhood, divorce.
- To give thanks and show appreciation.
- To create change, shift energies, and bring healing.
- To manifest a new job, new home or relationship, and so on.

Ceremony is a communal experience. It can be big or small and, as with all of our practice, intention is key. Plan, prepare and perform your ceremony from the heart. More guidance for group drum circles follows in the next chapter, but here are some pointers for you on ceremony:

Key Ingredients of Ceremony

- Strong intention
- Staying focused
- Solid preparation
- A clear safe space

- Creating a feeling of harmony and unity between yourself and the helping spirits
- Giving thanks

Preparation

Prepare Your Space: This includes ensuring it is energetically clear and also creating a sacred space with objects that have meaning for you. Items gathered from nature will hold the energy of the season and the landscape you are in, as well as the energy of all of those who are assisting. As you know, reiki is a wonderful tool for creating sacred space.

Prepare Yourself: Before the ceremony, you want to ensure you feel cleansed of stagnant energy so that you can fully receive and be present. Reiki and your drum can help with this, as can an Epsom salts bath. You may also like to wear special clothing like a scarf, hat or necklace as a way of stepping into non-ordinary reality for the ceremony. Or you may feel guided to create a mask, headdress or elaborate costume that also holds the energy of your intention. Make time for reiki before you begin, so you are focused and clear on your intention.

Prepare food and drink to help ground you at the end of the ceremony and share with others if they are present.

Prepare offerings and gather tools if needed, like drums and rattles.

Basic Ceremony Structure

- Prepare the space and open with a clear intention, ritual or song. (See suggestion on following page.)
- Cleanse the space, yourself and all participants.
- Present an offering to show your gratitude (the group can also beam reiki together).
- Call to the land, the elements and the directions to support the ceremony, and any other helping spirits who you wish to contribute.
- Hold hands with other group members to feel the flow of energy between you.
- Say prayers and blessings and send reiki to benefit all who are attending and radiate this out to the greater community, maybe even the whole planet.

- Create magic and harmony with song, chanting, drumming, dancing or sharing stories, jokes, poetry or reiki.
- Hold a clear intention and be guided; allow yourself to feel for what is needed in the space and allow the helping spirits to move through you.
- Close the space and express gratitude to all helping spirits.
- Ground yourself and others afterwards by sharing food, drink and merriment!

There is no right way for you to perform a ceremony! Simply set a clear intention and allow the power to flow. I can't emphasize enough the importance of tuning in to your own special way of knowing and sensing the right way for you to honour the natural environment that surrounds you. Do have a basic structure but don't get bound up in rules and instructions when engaging in ceremony; if you do then you will be only using your head. What is important is that you create something that has personal meaning for you. In this way the ceremony will strengthen your connection with both your inner spirit and the plants or natural world that you are inviting in.

Remember that ceremonies are not just to provide you with help and healing, they are a wonderful way to show nature, the plants and all the nature beings your appreciation and gratitude. In doing so, we help maintain high frequencies in the natural world, which in turn helps raise the vibration of our communities.

If unsure what to do, sit in *gassho* and invite reiki to flow, or play your drum and connect with a place in nature, your guide or a plant ally and ask for guidance; ask for what is needed and ask to be shown what that would look like. You may be shown an area of land that has lost its vibration and requires healing to bring it back to life, or you may simply feel that a ceremony to acknowledge and show your appreciation for your favourite place in nature is a perfect ceremony to start with.

Opening Space for Ceremony

There are many ways to open a space for ceremony or healing and you will already have your own methods within your reiki practice. What follows below is an example of how to welcome the energy of the directions with ritual, using your drum and reiki and the helping spirits. It really raises the energy when a group does this together. This example is influenced by my shamanic and Druidic training; work with it if it feels useful to you. You will need to know the compass directions before you begin, and you may wish to make a connection with them by journeying to each one in order to be shown what they represent. One person can lead the whole process, or different participants can represent each of the directions and take their turns speaking.

"We call to our ancestors, spirit guides, the spirit of reiki and the spirit of this land. We honour you and give thanks for your presence here in our ceremony and for holding your divine light in this space to keep us safe and protected for our healing here today."

The group turns to face the east; beat your drums and connect with the distance/connection symbol (*HSZSN*) and the power symbol to connect with the energies here. *"Spirit of the East we welcome you. Thank you for the beauty of new beginnings and the fresh perspective you provide. Thank you air for giving us the breath of life and all our winged and feathered friends."*

You may see colours or images, hear murmurs, feel sensations in your body, feel emotions or simply have a knowing of the resonance of the energies here. There is no right or wrong way to experience this.

Next, the group turns to face the south; everyone beats their drums and connects with the symbols as before to connect with the energies here. *"Spirit of the South we welcome you. Thank you for the creative fire and passion in our hearts. We give thanks to your power and the sun for giving us life."*

Pause in silence, then when you feel like you have connected with the energy here, move round to the next direction.

Turn to face the west; beat the drums as before. *"Spirit of the West we welcome you. Thank you for giving us the water of life and for helping us to experience our feelings. We are blessed with your presence today."*

Pause in silence, and when you feel like you have connected with the energy here, move round to the next direction.

Turn to face the north; beat the drums as before. *"Spirit of the North we welcome you. We honour the steadfast place of our ancestors and our resilience. Thank you, North, for being our guiding star."*

When you feel like you have connected with the energy here, bend to touch the Earth, kneel and beat your drums towards to Earth to connect with the energy here. *"Mother, we feel you, we honour you and thank you for everything that you provide; your constant support and nourishment in every action that we take. We honour and give thanks for every being that grows from your fertile land."*

Open to the Earth, feel yourself being held and your roots sinking down into the Earth. Drum with the heartbeat of the Earth. Then pause in silence.

Next, the group lifts their faces and drums towards the sky. Drum here to connect to the cosmos. *"Here we honour and give thanks to Father Sky, the moon and stars. Thank you for the light that you shine down upon me to light up my path. We honour and welcome the planets and star beings of the cosmos."*

Feel yourselves expanding up and out into the cosmos, held by the sacred web of life, connected to something so much greater. Pause to breathe all of this in.

Next, each person stands with hands on heart, tuning in to their heart centre; feel yourselves at the centre of the directions. *"We give thanks to the spirit that rests within each of us. We know that we are not confined to this physical body. We give thanks that we are not alone and are connected in the web of life to all things. We feel and honour this divine connection to the spirit that lives within all things."*

Drum together as a group here to honour each direction.

Now the space is open and you are ready to begin your ceremony or healing as per your intention.

Over time you will form your own relationships with each direction and the energies and elements present there. It can even be fun during a one-to-one session with a client to open the space together in this way. This helps clients participate in their healing and open to the energies and helping spirits that are present for them.

Healing with the Elements of Nature

Working with the elements of nature brings another dimension to your healing work, as each element brings a certain frequency and quality with it. You will find yourself naturally drawn to certain elements, like water or fire; this may change from season to season. We each have a unique combination of the elements alive within us and when they are in balance we experience health and harmony in our lives. The elements too are represented within the containers of the medicine wheel and the Celtic wheel of the year, which can be used to help create the sacred container for your practice. If you connect with the elements and get to know their qualities, you will have a deeper understanding of their power and how they relate to you.

To create your own relationships with the elements, as well as spending time physically with them you can undertake a drumming journey to meet them with your shamanic senses. In the journey space you can experience them differently; you can merge with them to experience their healing power and vibration. You may feel called to connect with different elements as part of a ceremony, for example as you work to clear and heal different issues.

TAKE ACTION Elemental Connection

Choose an element: earth, wind, fire or water. Preferably be beside that element, like next to the fire, out in the wind, by the water's edge, and hold in your heart the intention to get to know the element and its healing qualities and how they might help you in your practice as it develops. Invite reiki to flow (with the symbols if you like) and drum as you feel guided. Open yourself to receiving the energy of your chosen element. Notice how your rhythm flows and notice any physical sensations in your body or emotions. Enjoy this experience for as long as you need. Thank the element and other helping spirits that have accompanied you. Make notes accordingly about anything that feels significant.

Honouring Elemental Power

The power of the elements is often used to bring about transformation – such as a fire ceremony to help release thoughts and behaviours that are holding you back. A water ceremony might be created to cleanse away unwanted emotions and grief. As part of an earth ceremony, items can be buried in the earth to be transformed (such as a piece of paper with the names of those to be forgiven or released), or you can pile up rocks to create goals and dreams. We can also focus a ceremony on harnessing the power of the wind to help bring about change and transformation.

As you get to know the elements more deeply, you may also feel guided to share this with clients as part of a healing session. One way that I like to do this is by talking the client through a guided visualization using the slow, soft, steady beat of the drum as a background track. This not only helps a client relax but shifts their frequency and opens them up to the transformational power of the element. Depending on what a client needs, as your experience grows you may find yourself offering healing ceremonies for clients for deep-rooted issues with the help of the elements.

VISUALIZATION Water Cleansing Visualization

This is an example of a visualization with water to help a client be more receptive to healing. This visualization can be used at the start of a treatment to help release stagnant energy so that they can fully receive; or it could also be used as a stand-alone initial treatment with specific intentions of releasing and receiving.

Ensure your client is relaxed and comfortable on the treatment couch. Play your drum softly with a slow beat, inviting the client to relax a little more, breathing in and out, slowly, deeply. Visualize the waves on a beach gently coming into the shore and flowing out again.

You can also place the palm of your hand on the drum and stroke the drum to mimic the sound of the water.

Invite the client to let go of niggling thoughts and worries as they breathe out, and invite them to focus on their breath and the sound of the drum. Encourage the client to make sounds like sighs and yawns as they release. Invite the client to imagine that they are breathing in fresh *qi*, fresh vitality, and breathing out anything that is old and clunky. You may feel guided to drum over their body slowly or to simply stand back.

Invite them to affirm, "I am ready to let go of anything that is not serving me" or name something specific to them.

Describe to the client a spectacular waterfall with crystal-clear water that is vibrating next to them, with a magical diamond light that has the energy to transform, cleanse and recalibrate.

Invite the client to imagine and visualize that they are standing underneath this cleansing magical waterfall. Start at the crown – move here with your drum. Guide the client chakra by chakra, inviting them to allow the soothing, caring, cleansing power of the water into each energy centre. Move with your drum as you follow the cleansing water down each of the chakras. At each chakra, the water is cleansing, helping the client release as well as energizing and expanding the area. You may feel guided to name specific qualities, power, assistance and frequencies that the water is bringing into each of the client's energy centres.

Invite the client to allow this cleansing into each cell in their body, then, after you have reached the root, guide the client to bring their attention into the joints of the body, down their arms and legs, bringing ease, fluidity and flow. Visualize all that needs to be released flowing down through the body and into a river, pooling at the feet and joining a wider river for transformation. Speed up the drum with a flowing, expansive and energizing beat. You could also use the power symbol here.

Invite the client to think of one thing in their life that they would really like to release, something that they are truly done with carrying and wish to move on from. This could be a behaviour, a memory, an event they can't seem to get over. Invite them to give this up to the flow of this magical waterfall and drum down their body with the intention for this to be released. Then, ask your client to say out loud one area in their life where the high frequency of this beautiful water could bring more ease, joy and flow. Invite them to receive this with the whole of their being and drum accordingly.

When this feels complete, allow the client to rest in stillness for a few minutes, then give them reiki. You may feel that this has been a powerful experience and the client may not need a full session after all. When you want to end the session, give thanks to the spirit of water and make sure the client mindfully drinks water too.

Healing Your Wild

I used to find the concept of Wild Woman hard to relate to. It's not that I'm an overly good girl but I used to associate "wild" with reckless, careless, untrustworthy, devious, violent, angry, selfish and unsafe. It was an archetype that I didn't lean towards; rather I pushed away from it. What does the idea of Wild Woman (or Man) conjure up for you?

It wasn't until this was reframed for me by another shamanic teacher that the penny dropped and I finally understood and embraced this archetype. Wild Woman refers to your instinctive, intuitive, unconditioned, original nature. Doesn't that feel expansive? Your true nature, which is playful, sensuous, untamed and unashamed to be you. The Wild Woman is your natural, original state of being. There was huge freedom for me and a subtle but felt sense of relief in learning this, and it may be the same for you. It's time that the Wild Women and Men came out of the shadows. If you feel called, then experience this next journey to meet, heal and embrace the wild within you.

TAKE ACTION Journey to Meet Your Wild Woman (or Man!)

You may wish to experience this journey out in nature, or if that is too distracting then stay inside. Choose your preferred journey method. Maybe you wish to drum for yourself, listen to a drumming track or simply lie on the Earth, relax and breathe.

Hold in your heart your intention to meet the Wild Woman within you, and ask how she can be more present in your life. Prepare for your journey as you have already done countless times. Explore and enjoy. If after the journey you need further guidance, then don't hesitate to come back to the journey. Be sure to honour the Wild Woman that you find and to follow the whispers of the wild within you.

Wild Woman Journey November 2021

Hands are reaching for me,
Old hands, bony arms,
I land in the mud, the feeling is sensuous
I am held by the Earth, touched, cloaked by the mud
It feels fluid, damp.
I am birthing yet also
Dragging corpses with me as I go
The air is visceral, earthy, messy.
Wild.
I'm now in darkness, in a cave.
There is a light like an eye above me,
Watching over me,
I look up
A hand reaches in and picks me up
I land on the hand of my Wild Woman
Giant woman
She places me on her back
She carries me
I climb her hair up to her hat
So that I can see
But she tucks me safely into her breast
I feel warm and held
I snuggle and fall into her belly
Into my belly

Into the cosmic womb
What is the Wild Woman's message for me?
Run Free, she whispers
I hear this in my bones
I feel it on the wind
I see it in my dreams.

Reaching Up to the Heavens

Drumming out in nature, for the elements, plants, nature beings and spirits of the land, is a very grounding and embodied experience, as you open all of your senses to the natural world and feel your sense of connectedness. Reiki, however, by its very nature is otherworldly; it's intangible, etheric and mysterious. We can touch it and feel it within our body, mind and heart but not see it in physical form. Yet it is able to subtly move through our thoughts, feelings, words and actions and radiate high frequencies out into the world. In both my reiki and qigong practice I have always been shown that we (human beings) are pillars of light. We are connected both to the heavens (the divine and the greater cosmos) and to the Earth (our physical home). These two energies meet within us. When we invite reiki to flow, and relax, we can consciously open to this alignment.

Some people may feel a tingling at the crown of their head as reiki flows, or through their hands, even their feet. I visualize myself as a column of light, radiating out into the world. From my crown a beam of light reaches up to the heavens and from my root a beam of light reaches down into the Earth, aligning me with the energies of heaven and Earth. In both cases, the beam of light is both giving and receiving. I receive from the Earth and I also offer to the Earth; I do the same with the heavenly energies. My sense is that finding the balance between these two helps us live a purposeful, aligned and heart-centred life here on Earth that will help us to create the heaven on Earth that we long for. You don't want to be too "up there with your head in the clouds", otherwise your actions are not grounded in this earthly reality and it's hard to function. Conversely, if you are overly grounded, practical or materialistic you are stuck in a denser energy pattern that doesn't allow for the higher vibrations of the heavens.

As well as helping to feel the connectedness of nature, the drum can also assist you to expand your consciousness to experience the energies of the cosmos and beyond and come into a deeper relationship with them. Here are some suggestions to get you started.

TAKE ACTION Drumming to Bridge Heaven and Earth

I suggest doing this outside if possible. Prepare yourself in your usual way, inviting in your spirit helpers and reiki to flow. Hold your intention to connect with the energies of the heavens (the divine realms or upper world) and the Earth (lower world).

Close your eyes and pick up your drum. Focus on the heavens first. You may find yourself reaching up and drumming up towards the heavens. You may even feel yourself travelling upwards to the heavenly realms. Open to receiving this energy. Notice with your shamanic senses what you are receiving and what qualities it has. Make a sound as you drum that represents this energy. Feel it flowing over you through your crown and into your heart.

Then drum, calling yourself back down to Earth. You may find the power symbol useful here. Drum at your heart centre for a few minutes, feeling the expansion in your heart.

Next, turn your attention to your feet and connect to the invisible roots that anchor you into the earth. Drum yourself into the Earth to connect with the energies there. Drum, visualize or chant the power symbol to assist you.

Feel yourself travelling down and open all of your senses to this experience. Notice what you are receiving and how you feel. You may experience a physical sensation in your feet or throughout your body or notice a shift in your emotions. Make a sound as you drum that represents this energy. Feel it flowing up through your feet, up into your belly and into your heart.

Drum at your heart for a few minutes again to embody these two energies and honour them merging within you. See and feel yourself as a column of light bridging heaven and earth. Ask for a symbol or a word that represents this power and quality and how it can help you. Be open and notice what you receive.

When you feel complete, put down your drum and place your hand on your heart or your belly. Send yourself reiki to fully receive the energies of this session. Thank your guides and reiki when you are finished. Note down your experience. What has this shown you? How can you embody these energies more in your daily life?

Bridging heaven and Earth.

Cosmic Drumming

Any exercise in which you drum to connect with an aspect of the cosmos naturally feels expansive, inspiring and quite mysterious, since you really are connecting with the unknown. You can drum for many different reasons. At first you may like to drum to simply honour the sun when it shines and the life it brings. Or under stars in the night sky, with reiki, to show your appreciation. Drumming like this helps to create a conscious relationship between you and these cosmic elements that can be developed over time and woven into your healing practice. Shamanic journeys with a more specific intention can help you connect to the cosmos and gather further insights. For example, you can journey to merge with the energy of the moon and learn about the power of its different cycles, or drum to connect with a specific constellation or planet to discover more about its energy and influence on your life. The opportunities are as endless as there are stars in the sky. However, drumming like this is not just about ticking off these aspects of the cosmos from a list of "things I must journey to in order to …".

It's important to feel guided and ready to receive and act on any information or guidance that is offered to you. I have found that connecting with the cosmos and key elements of my astrological birth chart has given me a much broader perspective on me, my purpose and life on Earth in general. This can be especially helpful when making decisions or when experiencing challenges. It also really helps a sense of connection, perspective, compassion, awe and hope, because we truly are part of something expansive and amazing.

TAKE A BEAT

This chapter has aimed to inspire you to experiment with reiki and your drum out in nature (and the wider cosmos) to help you create connections between you and the natural world. This not only helps you feel supported and stronger but also reminds you who you truly are. You can do this most simply by drumming to honour and show your appreciation, or in a more elaborate way with specific, focused ceremony or daily rituals. As your connections are made and deepen, you are able to receive healing and wisdom from the natural world that surrounds you and may encounter allies for your life projects and healing work. Working with reiki and the drum is also a powerful way to send healing to those places and parts of nature where harmony needs to be restored. Offerings like this are often reciprocated and you will reap the benefits in your body, mind and soul. This chapter introduced ceremony, which is one way to bring a group together with a focused intention. Next, you're going to explore what to consider when bringing a group to drum together to experience the magic of the drum.

7

Drum Circles

While you will find great delight and deep personal joy in working alone with your drum, the power of a drum circle intensifies and magnifies the frequency of our intentions, prayers and healing. Gathering with like-minded souls who share in our values and can safely hold us as we work through our personal challenges to manifest our vision can feel supportive and like finding our true place in this world. There are many different styles of drum circle. They can be informal social and musical gatherings where each person in the group plays a percussion instrument and all repeat simple rhythms together. Or there are those led by an experienced facilitator in which participants receive healing, insight or relaxation from the drum, such as shamanic drumming, sacred ceremony, a sound journey, or a gong bath. My experience lies with the latter and so this is where my focus is for this chapter.

Many of us are instinctively drawn to attend drum circles, as if the beat of the universe was calling us home. I attended regular drumming circles with fellow shamanic and reiki practitioners from many traditions for about eight years before I finally surrendered to the nudge that was guiding me forwards to step up and lead myself. While I enjoyed the comfort of simply having to show up, connect, drum, listen, receive and be guided, I knew that leading my own groups was what was being asked of me and I had immense resistance.

The same is true for many of my students who suffer with the familiar inadequacies that originate from the song of the ever-protective ego, insisting that they aren't good enough, they don't know enough, don't have the confidence or can't do it. Part of the journey to holding the space for others is to compassionately face these fears as you step further into your light.

There is a great benefit in both attending a drum circle as a participant and holding the space as the space provider and circle organizer. In this chapter I'm going to talk you through some of the key points to consider when heeding the call to set up your own.

Meditation Becomes a Drumming Journey

Not long after my reiki Master Teacher Training and my reiki drum training, I started up a meditation class. The idea was to run a six-week course to share the techniques of breathwork and visualization that I had learned and that I found most useful to combat the rising stress from my 9 to 5. To my surprise, about six willing participants showed up ready to relax and receive my instruction.

After sharing several breathwork exercises with the group, I could see that many were struggling, very much caught up with the anxious thoughts that were going through their minds, and I could feel the frustration in the room. I knew in my heart what would help and I felt deeply called to play my drum.

After demonstrating the sound of the drum with the group I explained that I was going to softly drum and all they needed to do was to relax, take long, slow breaths and allow the beat of the drum to wash through them into their hearts and minds.

I called in my spirit guides and invited reiki to flow and started to drum. I was taken aback at how quickly the drum physically affected the participants. I could visibly see the shift, in the way that they were breathing, in their physical demeanour that appeared more relaxed and at ease and the sense of peace that was filling the room. I'm sure there was one participant who was on the edge of sleep.

At the end of the session the participants opened their eyes with a renewed sense of clarity and connection. It looked as if I had pressed a reset button somewhere in their unconscious minds. I felt like we had cheated. In a very short time, with the repetitive beat of the drum we had achieved the kind of deep relaxation that might often only be felt by an experienced meditator, not someone who has shown up for their first class.

After this I was hooked and full of admiration for the magnificent drumbeat. All of my classes from then on included a drumming session because I could see the benefits so clearly in the room and each participant could feel the relaxation, clarity and peace that the drum seemed to deliver.

Over the last twelve years my group experiences have developed from simple relaxation classes to deeper journey work for personal healing as my connection with guides, plants, new tools, techniques and ways of working deepens. While I no longer run meditation classes in this way, I still look back on these early experiences with a sense of wonder and know that it was the perfect way for me to begin.

Drum Circles: Where to Start

As you know by now, your intention is the magic that fuels the energy of your healing work and life. The same is true for your drum circles. Create the time and space for yourself to call in your sources of inspiration and guides to be with you, and ask to be shown what you need to know to help you create a drumming circle that will be healing for the group of people that you feel guided to invite.

The following are some reminders of what you need to consider.

Your Offering

Deciding what to offer is the first challenge and often means many practitioners fall at the first hurdle. You don't have to do this alone. Your guides can help you create an action plan. Be open to receiving insight about the themes, issues, clients, content, times, and location, to get clear on what you would like to offer. Taking notice of what you are being called towards will help you stay aligned with your joy and innate gifts. There may be a theme around issues that you repeatedly see your clients suffering with, such as relaxation, soothing grief or depression, energy restoration, or helping to release negative beliefs. You may wish to help inspire clients to achieve goals or manifest dreams. Or you may feel guided to theme your drumming circles around connecting with different seasonal energies, the moon, goddesses, plants, animal guides, and so on. The reiki drum can be combined with many offerings such as qigong, yoga, meditation, self-practice, gong baths, sister circles, and plant spirit and cacao ceremonies. My first group drumming sessions were not intended to be drum circles at all; the focus was on meditation and the drum was simply another tool that we used. Maybe this will be the same for you, allowing you to gently share the drum together with other practices, meditation, healing methods or sound instruments that you work with.

You may find that a specific guide steps forwards to assist you; be open to sources of inspiration and nudges from the universe. You may even find yourself starting before you feel ready. Jill, one of my students, was struggling with confidence when drumming for others until a friend invited her to drum for an equinox ceremony that she was holding. Jill wouldn't need to hold the circle, just step up and drum to help the participants relax for a short period of time. This invitation helped Jill overcome the anxiety and apprehension that has previously held her back; without this nudge from the universe, she might have procrastinated a little more about drumming for others, especially groups. Maybe you can find a fellow practitioner with whom you can collaborate and weave magic with drums, healing and sound together?

TAKE ACTION Creating the Feeling for Your Circle

Without thinking, note down your first responses to these questions. This will help you get a feel for what you are seeking to create.

1. List five things that make a good drum circle.
2. List five ways you want to feel before, during and after.
3. List five ways you want your client to feel before, during and after.

Look at your responses and notice any patterns, themes or what appears to be significant. Use these as pointers for keeping you on track as you plan your events. What I have noticed for myself and my students is that there is a delicate balance between the human – or I could say the practical – and the magical. A blend of these elements is essential for successful drumming events. The human needs of each participant like clear communication, knowing what to expect or bring or feeling safe and comfortable, are as important as the spiritual needs like wanting to feel connected and experiencing a sense of magic that they don't experience in everyday life. You will know what style works for you and find your own way to creating this harmony between the practical and the mystical.

Who Is Your Drum Circle For?

If you get clear on who your drum circle is for then it will be easier for you to work out the structure and the marketing, and then share information about what experience is required and what a participant might need to bring with them. You can appeal to specific groups like reiki practitioners, people with experience in sound journeys or shamanic practice. Or you can stay broad by aiming at complete beginners and people who are curious. If you already have a professional reiki practice then you will know your current client base well and inviting them will be a natural extension of your offerings. Having a clear idea of your drum circle participants is key to providing the right level of support, instruction and guidance before, after and during the circle.

It can feel daunting when other experienced therapists or teachers book to attend your reiki drum events. Your insecurities might kick in with fears that they might judge you – or worse still, steal all your best ideas! It helps to remind yourself that they are coming to RECEIVE and are usually so grateful that someone else is doing the hard work of organizing, holding space and running the show that their focus will be on themselves and not you! And remember, the more you trust in yourself and open to the guidance of your spirit helpers the more your offerings will carry that unique resonance that only you have.

Location

You will need to source a suitable location (where loud sound during the day or night is acceptable). One that is easy to reach with public transport or has good parking, is clean, warm and comfortable, as well as within your budget. Drum circles held outside are often a beautiful experience as they are supported by the elements and Earth energies; however, they are subject to the weather conditions and other sound influences such as lawnmowers and construction, and, if they are in a public place, may be interrupted by onlookers. So if organizing an outdoor drum circle, research your space well and always have a plan B.

Make sure you are able to view the venue at the time of day you will be holding your circle, and get clear on how long you are allowed access to the space in order to set up and clean up. Review facilities like the location of the toilets, where people can hang their coats, how to operate the heating or the air conditioning, what to do in case of fire, whether or not there is a kitchen or yoga mats provided, and note down what you might need to supply. If you like to burn incense or herbs or diffuse essential oils then clarify with the space holder that it's allowed – and make sure you know where the smoke detectors are!

When you have sourced a venue that feels good and meets your criteria, then drum to connect to the energies and the spirit of the place. Meet the spirit of the place, let them know what you are planning, ask to be shown the power of the place and what is needed. If you receive any guidance then make sure you act on it and honour the blessings you receive. You may feel guided to leave an offering, or to send reiki or healing prayers.

Tips for Holding a Drum Circle Online

Admittedly, this is not my favourite way of connecting people with the healing qualities of the drum; however, I am deeply grateful for the online streaming services that enable us to experience both reiki and the drum in real time from all corners of the globe. The advantages of such online spaces are obvious and you have most likely already experienced the amazement of being able to feel reiki and be part of a sacred healing space with others who are on the other side of the world. However, when we add in the sound component of the drum, online connection can get a little tricky and more unpredictable.

The first time I led a drum circle online I got so carried away with the drum that I made the mistake of moving away from my microphone; as a result, none of my eager participants could hear the transmission. It took me about twenty minutes to realize because I was so in the zone, by which time, unsurprisingly, many people had given up and dropped off the class. Oops. Don't make the mistakes that I have! Consider your equipment, the acoustics of the space from which you will be drumming, and make sure you have the correct audio settings on your computer and the online service that you are using. It may be worth investing in a microphone rather than making use of the inbuilt one that comes with your computer. As a very general rule, the more you pay for kit, the better the sound quality of the microphone will be. It's also worth doing a sound check so that you know how near to the microphone you need to be for optimum sound and how strongly you can beat your drum before the sound distorts. You will also need to know where to look so that participants will see you looking at them directly. Sadly, no matter how good your equipment, set-up and preparation, if your internet connection or the internet connection of your participants is poor, then the sound quality will distort.

It can feel challenging in the online space to gain rapport and generate the energy for the energetic container, particularly if participants do not turn on their cameras. This certainly doesn't help with the nerves either! During in-person circles you can look each other in the eyes and it's easier to feel the energy of others and feel supported by it. To help you through this online, you may find that you need to be a little more light-hearted and make use of icebreakers to help the group bond. You may also find it useful to surround yourself with high-frequency objects that strengthen you, so they can support your energy. I also recommend a warm sage tea (or other herb that supports the throat), or water, so that you take care of your voice.

When I offer online drum spaces, as well as the above checks I also make sure to drum quite softly, with less exuberance than I would if the group was in-person. In this way, I make sure that the sound has minimal opportunities to come over in an unacceptable way. However, this restrained way of drumming doesn't feel that authentic to me, which also brings its own issues. In my experience of the online streaming platforms, the loudest sounds present are those that the group hears; for this reason I have not had much success in instances in which each member is drumming with me. The only way I have managed this is by placing all participants on mute and having myself as the main drummer. This way, each participant can hear both their own drumbeat and the beat of my drum but none of the other sound. If online circles appeal to you and you feel confident with the tech, then experiment and play with different settings and ways to make your drum circle harmonious and authentic. I would be excited to hear from you!

Receiving or Participating?

Will you be drumming alone as you offer the healing sound of the drum and reiki to your participants as they lie down to receive, or will your participants be actively drumming with you? Or maybe a mix of the two? If participants are showing up to simply receive then they won't need to bring their own drum, they can simply show up willing and ready to experience. You can offer this to beginners or those with more experience journeying with sound. It can be fun for participants to actively experience the power of the drum by participating in the whole or part of the drumming circle. For example, participants can be invited to drum, rattle or make sound as you open the space and call in your guiding spirits and helpers. This can really help raise the energy of the circle. When you have more experience in holding space for others, you may also invite participants to drum with you rather than passively receive. However, to do this it is likely that they will need their own drum. Tune in and ask for guidance on what feels right to offer.

What Does the Participant Need to Know in Advance or Bring with Them?

It's worth spending a few minutes thinking about the key questions that clients might ask about the drumming experience and how you can answer those. What's the experience going to be like? How is it going to make them feel? What happens during the session? Information like this may already be included in your marketing about the event. It can also be beneficial to link to a video so that clients can hear a sample of the sound and visually take in what a drum circle might look like. Provide a list of what a participant must bring with them; this often includes items such as water bottle, yoga mat, blanket, eye mask, or maybe their own drum or rattle. If your location has quirks or specific instructions to follow then make sure these are communicated clearly. Also consider what you need to know about your clients. If they were coming for a one-to-one treatment you would require that they complete a client record form, so it is good practice to ask for this in group situations too. That way you will have a record of their health issues, their consent and relevant contact information. This can be done online in advance of the class; and if they have not all been completed before the class starts, you can have some printed copies available for participants to complete on the day.

Marketing Your Event

Your current client base, if you already have one, will be the ideal audience to help you start out. I have found that clients often like to come to a group drum circle before investing in a one-to-one session. If you don't have an existing client base then work out the minimum number of people you need to make the session viable for you and consider where to find the people who your circle is aimed at. Social media or specific event platforms are obvious places to share your event, but nothing beats in-person interactions, word of mouth and old-fashioned posters and flyers. It can feel overwhelming to know what information to put in your marketing, so I have a simple tip for you:

TAKE ACTION Marketing Blurb

In order to attract the right audience for your drumming circle, it helps to be really clear about who your circle is for and what's in it for them. This not only helps hone your marketing message but also makes it easier for you to focus on your intention and create your powerful session.

List all the ways that your drum circle will benefit your participants. Look at your list. Which of these are specific to the group that you are marketing to or the theme of your session? And how can you make them more specific?

For example, lying on the sofa can feel relaxing, so what is it about reiki drumming with you that makes it more beneficial than that?

Is there an issue that could be solved, alleviated or clarified?

What kind of transformation could the session bring that is specific to your audience and means something to them?

Leave your mind mulling all that over for a while, then come back to it later that day and pick your top three that stand out and feel most important to your audience. Stick with these as part of your marketing copy and message.

How Much to Charge?

Many practitioners find it difficult to price their offerings, and more often they fall into the trap of undercharging rather than overcharging. Unless you are hosting a charity fundraiser or are happy to receive donations, you are running a business and you need to get practical about your fees. Consider the cost of the room hire, the time you spend preparing, and any costs of marketing or materials.

Think about the number of people your venue can hold and you are happy holding space for. You will need to calculate the minimum number of places that you need in order to run your event and cover your costs. Getting clear on what your drum circle is offering and how it benefits the participants can make it easier to price your event. Of course, you will naturally compare yours with the price of other similar events, but remember your offering is unique and it is up to you to successfully communicate that message. There are also many sales tactics you can use, like introductory or early-bird offers.

Ahead of Time

Plan your session and get clear on what you are offering and who it is for. Let the world know and gather folk in the way that feels most aligned with you. Social media can be very effective for sharing your events and showing snippets of you and your drum.

Always ask for guidance from your guides and also from the place where you will be holding your circle.

Make sure you are clear on what you need to bring with you. Make a list rather than simply gathering everything together on the day. I still use a very old list from years ago that details the items that I need to have with me (yes, it even includes my drum!).

Send reiki or healing light ahead of time to your events so that no matter how rushed you are, or nervous when the circle is starting and going ahead, you can rest assured knowing that reiki is holding the space with you, for the highest good of all beings.

Make sure your participants know what time you are starting and what time they can arrive. It can be tricky and distracting if you are trying to set up your space when students are arriving and are excited to chat to you. Decide how you will manage this. If you benefit from quiet time to prepare your space, create that for yourself by giving clients a time that they can enter the room from and not before.

On the Day

Arrive early – with everything you need. Clear your space energetically and set up the room how you like. I always set up an altar space with candles, seasonal elements, elements of the medicine wheel, my tools and instruments, crystals and oracle cards.

Prepare yourself – make sure you give time to allow yourself to breathe, get grounded and get connected to your guides and your intention. It can help to have an item of clothing, like a scarf, robe or belt, or jewellery, like a pendant, that is a sacred item that you only wear during your reiki drum or healing spaces. You can put this on before you begin as a sign that you are leaving behind non-ordinary reality and entering in sacred space, and remove it at the end as a sign that your work is done.

Be clear on how you will manage payment (maybe people have to pre-book online) and how you will manage late arrivals or no-shows. Welcome your participants, get everyone settled in and begin (on time).

The Get-Out-Of-Jail Plan

Maybe a better way to put this is to talk in terms of safety. When your clients gather in circle, some of them will be new to you, new to the drum and have no idea what to expect. The majority of the time, everyone will relax to the sound of your drum and drift off into the dreamtime for a healing adventure. Every once in a while, someone will feel really unsettled by your drum, either with emotional release or with physical symptoms like nausea. With this in mind, I like to offer my participants what I call the get-out-of-jail card (I don't actually share this name!). What this is is permission to leave the space. When I introduce them to the drum, its sound and where I will use it, I let them know that if at any time they feel uncomfortable, they can raise their hand and I won't approach them with the drum. Plus, if they really feel uncomfortable, they can leave the room and step outside (quietly and without disturbing others). I reassure them that this is OK and that even outside the room, they will be receiving what they need.

I also reassure them that reiki is working for the highest good of all beings. Think about whether you feel guided to do this too. In the last fourteen years, I've only had two people walk out of the room. I give this permission so that participants don't feel trapped. The exception for this is when I am holding a ceremony; during a ceremony it feels important that everyone stays in the circle to hold the space and share the experience, so I don't offer ceremony participants this option.

If you know that you might get nervous, it's helpful to create a plan with timings so that you don't forget anything and so you stay on track. You don't need to stick rigidly to the plan (and often the energy may not let you!), but it can be useful and reassuring for the mind to know that you have one, even though when you get going the spirit of reiki, the drum and your guides will take over. The following is a guideline that you might find useful to base your own drumming circle or session around.

Drum Circle Guidelines

Open the space, call in the directions, your guides and helpers and reiki. (You may like to use the opening space example in the previous chapter, page 144.)

Give your welcome and introduction, explain the flow of the session and share a little about you.

If time allows, invite each participant to introduce themselves and share what brought them here today.

Share the intention or theme of the circle – give an explanation if relevant, i.e., if you are connecting with a specific season or goddess, you may wish to share what this means to you and others may like to do the same. Share the sound of your drum if relevant and include the get-out-of-jail plan if you wish.

Invite everyone to get comfortable. Often for healing circles this looks like each person lying down on a yoga mat or lounge chair with a blanket to cover them and an eye mask or scarf to cover their eyes. You may like to have extra cushions available to put under knees.

Explain to the participants what will happen during the session and what they need to do. Invite them to relax and receive and to allow the drum to penetrate their body and take them on a journey.

Lead a short meditation or guided visualization with the drum or with music, and beam reiki if appropriate. I find this useful to relax participants prior to working with the drum and the specific intention of the circle. It gets everyone in a relaxed space from which it's easier to connect with the drum.

Begin the main drumming piece relating to the circle's intention. Work with the drum and/or other tools. You may like to walk around the participants and drum over specific areas of their bodies, or you may stay in one place by your altar or at the centre. Walking around can give a personalized approach and feel to the session; however, if you have many participants or space is limited then this is not practical. I have sadly mis-stepped on people by mistake and it's not the most relaxing experience for a participant – though a gentle nudge with your foot can be handy if there is a loud snorer in the circle who you feel may be disturbing the others.

When you feel the session is complete, be clear that it is finished and give the participants space and time to come back into this reality. You may wish to guide them by talking them through gentle stretches or a visualization, or leave them to slowly move their body. If your clients are reiki practitioners you may invite them to self-practise and place their hands on areas of the body where they feel guided. Alternatively, you might like to offer reiki to participants individually.

Play integration music to help this process, beam reiki to the group and remember to listen for guidance yourself. If they are all reiki-attuned you could also include a group sharing circle holding hands.

Invite everyone to sit up, so that you can see their faces and know that they are back. You may like to call in the power symbol and lead them through a grounding meditation to ensure they are back in material reality.

If time permits, the sharing of herbal tea and snacks like chocolate, nuts or fruit can also ensure that participants are ready to face the world.

At the end of a circle, participants may feel sleepy and not really able to express in words their experience. Offering everyone an oracle card can help bridge the internal experience with the outside world and offers a few talking points with extra insight. Sharing is an art; you don't want to pressurize the group to share if they don't want to or don't feel ready. You also want to be very clear about how much time the group has for sharing. It's hard to cut someone off when they are in full flow because you are looking at the clock, especially if you weren't clear beforehand about the length of time they had to share. If I am pressed for time, I will invite the participants to share a word that sums up how they are feeling or briefly share one thing they are grateful for, rather than take up the time with many stories. This is often sufficient for a short circle; you can use more in-depth sharing spaces at longer events. It can be useful to ask participants how they are feeling and compare this to how they felt at the beginning. The most common shifts are from tired, anxious, frustrated to energized, relaxed, peaceful or similar. Reinforcing this transformation and benefits helps people realize and remember the benefit of coming to reiki drum circles, so that hopefully they will return! If experiences have been very deep or emotional, then participants may not want to share right away; in these cases it can feel supportive to let them know that you are available after the session if they need to talk to you about their experience; or indeed that you can offer one-to-one experiences to assist them further.

Answer any questions, give thanks and close the space.

Make sure you yourself are grounded! Then clean up and leave.

NOTES ON CEREMONY: The structure of a ceremony (for me) differs slightly in a number of ways to that of a drum circle, as laid out above. Firstly, any explanations of what will happen are detailed beforehand so when we open the space, we are already in the energy of the intention. Another difference is that when I work in ceremony, I don't include introductions at the beginning or sharing at the end. Perhaps after the ceremony is completed the group might gather in a circle with a cup of tea to share anything that feels relevant. However, often ceremonies can feel very powerful and personal, so I find that holding and allowing these experiences to settle within ourselves can be more useful than automatically sharing with (giving it away to) others. As already explained, I don't offer participants the get-out-of-jail card here either, so once the ceremony begins it is agreed that the group stays together. I find that ceremonies generally involve more participation from the group as each of them may be involved in a process, whereas a drum circle can be simply for a participant to lie back, receive the drum and be guided on a journey. You will make your own choices about what works and what is required. Revisit the previous chapter for the ceremony guidelines to help you create your own magical healing spaces (page 142).

Ungrounded and Unaware

The first time I held a drumming circle for a substantial number of people was part of a women's retreat in Nova Scotia. I was one of many practitioners who were offering our services. We had no idea exactly how many would show up to our individual sessions; it was a case of being there for whoever joined you. On the schedule right before my own session was a journey dance session, so I gladly participated to get myself in the mood.

After the session I felt elated and energized. I quickly took a deep breath and large gulp of water before picking up my drum and opening my own space. Many of the journey dance participants stayed for my session and we were struggling for space on the floor as yoga mats were shifted to make room for everyone to lie down and get comfortable. There were around thirty participants. Thirty different energies for me to hold in that unfamiliar space that I had never been to before. I began as I usually do and ran the session smoothly. I remember finding it hard to hold (why didn't I call in more guides for support? my experienced self asks me now). I also remember hearing the drum reverberate strangely in some areas of the room. (Why hadn't I played it here and tested it out before the session? my experienced self asks me now.) I held on and closed the space as I usually do, answering questions and listening to feedback. The next session in the space was due to start, so we were ushered out abruptly. The energy was high, perhaps a little frantic, the room was buzzing. Were my feet even on the ground? Probably not.

This was my last session, the participants had quickly departed and so it was time for me to head home. Rather foolishly, in my haste to get back I just jumped in the car. I should have realized when I took a wrong turn out of the car park and had to reverse that I wasn't in a fit state to drive. It took me another few minutes to wake up and come back to reality. What was I doing? Why was I driving? And where was my drum?

It was at that moment of realization that I had left my drum that I knew I was not grounded and I was certainly not fit to drive a car. Fortunately, living in rural Nova Scotia, I wasn't yet on a main road. I pulled over, got out of the car and placed my feet on the Earth.

That was the first and last time I have left a drum circle ungrounded and the ONLY time I have been so not-on-this-planet that I have forgotten to pick up my beloved drum!

Let this never happen to you! Always ensure that you and your participants are all safely back and grounded on the Earth after a session or a drumming circle. If a client has to drive make sure they have a cup of tea, stamp their feet on the Earth, eat some chocolate, breathe deeply into their bellies.

After the Drumming Has Settled

As you know, the drum is a powerful tool and has the ability to create change and initiate deep transformation even after just one session. Be prepared for this! Consider how you can support your participants after your drum circle. If you are offering short events with a focus on rest and relaxation, you might feel this is not necessary; however, if you are offering longer, deeper healing ceremonies, you may find that participants need extra support and healing sessions as part of their journey to help integrate any feelings that have surfaced.

Often when our sessions come to a close, participants can still be reflective, processing the experience. They may not even realize until the day after the session that they have a question, an issue that needs further attention or a desire to share their experience. As you get to know your clients and the depth of your healing work, you will get to know what level of support feels right to offer. Some practitioners have online groups where participants can ask questions or share experiences, others offer discounted one-to-one sessions to support clients with integration.

As always, even though you are the practitioner who is holding the space, the group sessions will be healing on a certain level for you also. Make sure that you give yourself the time and space to integrate fully, and seek further assistance and self-treat with reiki if the experience has triggered you in any way.

Ideas and Themes for Healing Drum Circles

To get you started on what you can theme your drum circle around, the following may inspire you. However, before you read on, I suggest you list ten ideas that you already have for your drumming events and pick your top three. Add to your ideas with any of those suggestions below, notice which themes light you up and always choose what feels most aligned with you, rather than what you feel you ought to do.

- To relax and release stress
- To energize
- To heal a past experience/trauma
- To connect with the ancestors
- To feel nurtured and loved
- To meet a guide, a power animal or a plant spirit
- To receive healing
- To receive inspiration and unblock creativity
- To release a limiting belief
- To learn more about reiki and awaken your inner healer
- To shift a negative thought pattern or behaviour
- To connect with seasonal energy
- To connect with the elements
- To work with the reiki principles
- To manifest a dream or vision
- To experience a ceremony

Once you have narrowed down your ideas, you can journey with your drum or sit in *gassho* to ask for further guidance. I also sometimes might journey around deciding between different dates or locations. Don't try to ask, "which one is better?"; instead ask to be shown the outcome of one, and then the outcome of the other. You can then decide which one feels right for you.

TAKE ACTION **Drumming to Bring Momentum into Your Drum Circles**

From your sacred space, with reiki and your helping guides around you, visualize yourself holding your drum circle. In your mind's eye walk yourself through the process from receiving client bookings, to the set-up, welcoming participants, holding the space and seeing the shift that occurs for participants at the end of your session. Paint a vivid picture, include sounds like comments or questions you would like to hear. Make it feel as real and as wonderful as you intend for it to be.

Next, pick up your drum and play a rhythm to send reiki to energize and bring momentum into your event. Work with the symbols or create an affirmation if that feels right. When you feel complete, stop drumming and allow the experience to integrate by playing a piece of music and self-treating with reiki. Be open to any further guidance you receive.

TAKE A BEAT

The drumming circles that I have held over the years have been truly diverse and from one extreme to the other. I've held healing circles in living rooms, yurts, tiny back rooms, offices, public parks, my back garden, school classrooms, as well as fully kitted out yoga studios. I've held circles for large groups as part of larger gatherings and I've held circles for two.

I even had one occasion where no one showed up because those who had pre-booked all forgot to come. It was just me and my drum and that was just how it was meant to be. I've drummed in the snow, the rain and (thankfully) the sun. If the drum is calling you then allow its beat to flow through you and call to others. Your circle will take the form that fits the container that you have the capacity to hold and it will morph and grow over time with your practice and the assistance of your guides. If at any stage you don't feel sure of what to do, then invite reiki to flow, pick up your drum and play. The inspiration will flow.

Developing Your Drum Practice

◎ ◎ ◎ ◎

Like reiki, drumming is simple. With reiki you invite it to flow with your intention, whereas with the drum you pick it up and strike a beat. However, as you will have no doubt discovered in your reiki practice, your level of sensitivity and knowing increases the more you practise and experience reiki, and the same is true when you work with your drum. A book, a course, a certificate; these, valuable though they can be, are just the start of your journey. You will learn more through your own direct experience and your relationship with your guides, not via someone else's ideas.

In the last fourteen years, since I have been practising shamanic reiki, I have noticed a great number of changes in the way that shamanic techniques are taught, received and adopted by students. It feels like the old models of learning are falling away and it's up to us to forge new pathways as we bring guidance and wisdom through in ways that feel aligned with our truth.

Guided by reiki, your drum and your spirit helpers, you will find that you are intuitively led towards practices and techniques that feel right and you will develop your own style of connecting to the expanded worlds that the drum leads you to and how this can shape your gifts as a healer. The principal factor that I see holding back both reiki and shamanic students from reaching clients with their drum in professional practice is lack of confidence. While the ego often wants to learn more techniques because it claims that what you currently know is not enough, the truth is that you already have everything you need for success. Playing your drum solo, in groups, for clients, out in nature or with your dog is a sure way to get the experience that you need to and increase your confidence. In this chapter I wanted to share some more guidance and processes that you may find useful along the way to help you hone your skills and dive deeper into the mystery. As always, make use of those which you feel a natural gravitation towards; you can always circle back to other exercises at a later date.

Self-Care

As the container for your practice, in order to keep your light vibrant so that you can hold space for others it's vital that you take practical steps to look after your energy and keep it clear. Self-care is a rather overused term and there are numerous strategies and practices, many of which can seem obvious or patronizing. What's important is that you know what nourishes and nurtures you. Make use of reiki techniques that strengthen your energy and keep you grounded, and self-treat with reiki.

Ensure that you invite in protection when you are working with your drum and that you disconnect from the energies of clients, places or situations, and difficult issues when you have been doing healing work.

Cultivate your connection to nature and the everyday nonsense things that bring you joy and keep you sane. You are spirit personified, having a human experience, so as much as it is exciting, revelatory and healing to journey into the shamanic worlds or be in your reiki meditative space, it is also the greatest opportunity to be here on Earth alive and in this moment. Spirit guides can be loving, full of wisdom and supportive; however, sharing a pot of tea with a like-minded friend and setting the world to rights can also feel that way. Relish the sensations, feelings and surprises of the adventure of being alive. Delighting in the small joys that awaken your senses and touch your heart helps you to be in the vibration of gratitude. Be in the now and love the human experience for what it is. Do you need to make everything a spiritual experience or can some things be fun, frivolous, silly and utter nonsense? Find your balance.

Holding clear boundaries is part of your essential self-care. This means knowing what is acceptable for you, what you are and what you are not available for, and not being afraid to state it. Friends, family and some clients can be our greatest teachers, and can trigger us and act as the catalyst that makes us set clearer boundaries and have the courage to say no (nicely). Being clear about your boundaries will also help you as you navigate the spirit world, meet different guides and become more open to spirit messages. As a reiki healer, you have a bright loving light that acts like a beacon for many other beings and may attract attention. You can set the dial about what you are available for and what you are not available for during a journey or treatment. For example, if you are working with a client then you can state as part of your intention that this is the only healing you are available for in that session. This ensures that there is a clear boundary that does not include any other soul that might be attracted to the healing light of the session. This is all part of setting up your clear space and always holding a clear intention. If you are very intuitive and receptive to energies, you may wish to also let your guides know what times are OK for this to happen and when it's not appropriate. You do have to function in the human world and it's not helpful to have spirit showing you things when you are navigating traffic on the motorway.

Make sure you have your touchstones and sanctuaries, people, activities and places that keep you aligned with what you know is true for you and what feels right in your heart. Most of all, show compassion to yourself. Of all of the reiki precepts, this one is the greatest challenge and the one that I feel needs most of our attention. Peace, kindness, love, forgiveness and compassion start with ourselves and radiate out into the world. Be patient with yourself, treat your inner shaman like a toddler who is learning – or rather, re-learning. You are remembering your connection with spirit and your shining truth and power. Your growth won't come when it is forced, under pressure or contracted. It is only when you can hold that open, non-judgemental and compassionate space for yourself that you can hold that space for others to also heal. Meditating or drumming with the harmony symbol can be helpful, as can asking yourself the simple question, "What's the most loving thing I can do for myself right now?" Taking the time to celebrate you, the wonder that you are and all your wins, great and small, is another way to maintain the flow of love, light, joy and gratitude that holds you in your vibration of truth and power. If there are achievements in your life that you feel have gone unseen, then bring them into the light with ceremony, healing and gratitude so that more blessings can join them.

TAKE ACTION Soothing Anxiety with Reiki and the Drum

For this healing with the drum, rather than play the drum with your beater, I suggest cradling it in your arms and softly tapping out a heartbeat on the drum head. If you have a small drum, you may like to hold it over your heart. It can also feel comforting to sit cross-legged on the floor to feel the support of the Earth from beneath. Alternatively, leaning with your back against a tree will also help you feel comforted and held. Having a bunch of roses with you will also help invite in compassion and love.

Create a sacred space, connect to reiki and your drum and feel your intention in your heart as you drum. Drum softly and tenderly, feeling the drum with your hands. You may even like to stroke the drum head, as if treating it in a nurturing and caring way like it is a truly precious being that needs comforting (the drum is you, so show it how much you care).

Work with the symbols if you are guided. Whenever I work with emotional issues I always support them with the harmony symbol and the power symbol together.

You may also feel like expressing your emotions through your voice, so let yourself make sound as you drum. Or you may simply find yourself sighing and releasing with your breath.

It may feel right after drumming for a while to put down the drum and self-treat with reiki as you play a short piece of soothing and uplifting music.

Journal afterwards to reflect on this healing and what other support you can find to help you feel less anxious.

Cradling the drum and playing with your hands, whether for yourself or someone else, can feel soothing.

Journeying Deeper

Over time you may find your journey process shifts. At first you may find that the classic structure outlined in Chapter 3 suits you well and enables you to explore the shamanic worlds in a safe way. However, as you become more confident and begin more and more to trust your guides to help you, you may find that your journey process, or the way that you connect with guides and are shown information, changes. For me, I started out learning the journey process by lying down with a blindfold on and listening to drumming tracks. Today you have much more at your fingertips. You can personalize your tracks by recording yourself drumming on your phone or computer without the need for complex gadgetry.

I learned the journey process way before I owned a drum, but it was certainly the process that got me hooked so that purchasing my first drum was inevitable. Lying down to listen to a drumming track can seem like a passive process and you may find yourself giving yourself self-reiki during the journey. For this reason you may feel that actively drumming for yourself and taking yourself on a journey process while drumming suits you more. Though this can also take practice, if drumming for yourself, you may find that the initial structure of the journey fades away and you simply allow yourself to be guided.

Over time my journey practice has shifted and I often find myself turning to nature to request a sign, whether walking in nature or sitting next to a tree to receive information from guides that I might in the past have requested as part of a drumming journey. Be open to how your journey process may change and stay open to guidance from spirit that will nudge you.

When you feel like you have got the knack of journeying for yourself with the drum, you may feel like an explorer who is on a quest to find out information on the universe and everything. Try not to confuse yourself by doing too many journeys at once. Not only can this muddle you and leave you ungrounded, but it leaves you with not much time for allowing the experiences to integrate and for you to put into action any of the guidance that you may have received. As well as journeys to help your clients, when you have developed a relationship with a trusted guide you can journey with them to explore solutions to those challenges and questions that you hold in your heart.

Here are some suggestions for reiki-related journeys that I continue to find insightful and interesting:

- Journey to meet Usui or another Master or teacher in your reiki lineage to ask a question about reiki and healing or to receive a symbol to use in your practice.
- Journey to the future you to ask what you need to know now about your reiki practice.
- Journey to ask to be taken to a point on your timeline that requires healing.
- Journey to your shadow to heal the part that is ready.
- Journey to your crystals or other tools to find out more about how to work with them in self-healing or for specific clients.
- Journey with each of the reiki precepts to ask for deeper insight about how to apply them in your life.
- Journey with each of the reiki symbols to experience their power.
- Journey to Mount Kurama (where Usui first experienced reiki), to meet the spirit of the mountain.

Honouring Your Ancestors

Your ancestors are your spiritual heritage. You hold their wisdom, memories and experience within your DNA. I have found that when we begin to acknowledge them, we start to feel a little more whole within ourselves, and we may also experience a positive change in living family members. It's not that we need to know who our ancestors were or what they experienced, it's more about honouring today the energy of the lineages that created you. You are the sum of those souls in those lineages, together with any other lives that you have incarnated as. For many of us, feeling the presence of a loved one who has passed away, like a grandma, may be our first experience of connecting with the spirit world. There are many ways to honour those who walked this Earth before you with ceremony, celebration, photographs, sharing stories and mementos. You can also drum to journey to connect with your ancestors to receive guidance and healing. This can be particularly beneficial if you feel the loss of a loved one or feel guided to send healing to a specific area of your lineage. For any journey that connects through time and space to the ancestors, I will always drum with the distance/connection symbol as well as the harmony and power symbols.

If you or a client are having difficulties following the loss of a loved one, then holding a ceremony with the intention to honour their life and release them can be a healing experience as part of the grieving process when the time is right.

TAKE ACTION Journey to Connect with Your Ancestors to Ask for a Blessing

Prepare yourself and your space and spend a few minutes in quiet reflection considering those who went before you. If there is a spccific relative or side of the family that you wish to connect with then make that your intention. Otherwise hold a general intention to connect with your ancestors and receive a blessing for your work. Drum with reiki and the symbols when you are ready, and enjoy the expansive connection to the ancestors. Be open to receiving their blessing. This may come as a symbol, a word, an emotional response or physical sensations in your body. Beam them your gratitude and close down your space when you are complete. To anchor this experience on Earth in this reality, go outside and choose a tree to be with. Send the tree reiki or simply connect and allow the blessing to flow through you into the tree. Reflect on how you can bring in more of the support of the ancestors into your life.

The End of Life

The end of life is a sensitive and delicate time, and not just for the person who is about to transition; its effects ripple out across family and loved ones through generations. Anxiety, fear, regret, anger, sadness, helplessness, blame, guilt, despair and loss are but a few of the range of emotions and reactions that may surface at this potentially fraught time. To make matters even more challenging, the end of life is not a widely discussed subject in our culture, so our suffering is often hidden or repressed. Working with the drum and reiki can bring in love, support and relief for all of those who are affected at such a difficult time.

Drumming with reiki for someone who is passing can also be a way to support their transition and guide them home. Since the nature of this work is sensitive and individual, my sense is that you don't need to go looking for opportunities to work in this way. Rather, if you are meant to support people at the end of their life, then you will be guided to do so.

Soul Pieces

Often when I strike out a rhythm on my drum, it's as if the beat calls forward pieces of me. These are soul parts or shadow aspects that have been forgotten, pushed away, ignored, hidden in shame, buried in guilt, left abandoned, stolen by places, people and events throughout time. Sometimes I might be able to name them or find that they bring with them a twinge of something remembered, other times I might not be able to label what these fractured soul parts are, but the drumbeat creates what feels like a sense of completion and wholeness in my being. It feels as if more of me is now available to me than before. This can often be emotional and even blissful and is always expansive. You may find that the drum does the same for you. Be open to the soul fragments from this lifetime and beyond that the drum may be returning to be with you in the here and now. If you are drawn to soul retrieval work like this, you may find that further training is useful to help you integrate these pieces of you and assist others with this type of healing. Though I myself have received specific shamanic training in soul retrieval techniques, it is through experience with reiki, my drum, my clients and my guides that I have built on this understanding and developed my own way to hold this healing. If you are called to this type of work or if you feel there is a part of yourself that is stuck in time, leaving you feeling like something is missing, there are a number of ways you can explore this process for yourself. The starting point would be to sit in *gassho* and meditate or to undertake a journey and ask to be shown a soul part that is ready to come back. I would also suggest that you journey to invite a guide to come forward that will help you with this type of healing and to show you how they can help. If you feel ready to invite this part of you back, then ask your guide to help you with the process. A key part of soul retrieval healing is the integration of your soul part coming back home to you, which is where the light and love of reiki will tenderly support you. As well as self-reiki practice or reiki meditations you may also find journaling useful, to acknowledge your feelings.

The drum may also help us become aware of our shadow (parts of our personality and behaviour that we try to ignore, hide, deny or are ashamed of for example). Again, through communication with your guides, you can choose to work on specific areas or ask to be shown what you need to bring into the light. Shadow work can be uncomfortable and emotional as those hidden parts of you become seen and receive the love that they are calling for. Reiki will be a nurturing and supportive love and light that holds you through the process while the drum and your guides call those pieces of you home and heal the resistance to their acceptance. The beauty of combining the drum with reiki is that we know and trust that reiki will cause no harm. So when you are called to explore those deep and often painful parts of yourself or your experiences, you know you are supported for your highest good and that of all beings. In this sense reiki not only provides the light, love and healing frequency, it also assists us with the courage that drives our path of self-healing and quest for truth, balance and peace.

Your Soul's Mission

How often do you doubt yourself in what you are choosing in your life or how you are making your living? Are you waiting for that giant download that comes in one day during a reiki session that takes you step by step through the process of what you need to do in order to fulfil your soul's purpose or life mission? For most of us, I don't think it really works that way. Do you ever follow those who are seemingly doing their life's work, only to get an email from them a few months later saying that they have shifted gears? It happens, right? We are each evolving and listening to the nudges and whispers of the universe, trying to follow the flow of those things that bring us joy. Sometimes we don't listen well enough, and resist a change until life decides for us and we are forced onto an unknown path. Sometimes we are so shut down from our soul's voice that we drift from one thing to another, or we are trapped into conforming to expectations and do what we "should" do, denying what we would love to do. Many people find themselves on their reiki path because they felt called to it. I believe that reiki guides us to reveal that light of truth within us, that spark that is uniquely us. Simply being in that vibration of you is your mission on Earth. Learning reiki enables us to *be* reiki (being ourselves), and it doesn't mean that you have to give reiki to others as a professional practitioner. Likewise, shamanism too is a calling. In traditional shamanic cultures, there are specific initiation processes that bring the apprentice to the shaman. We are fortunate that we can work with many shamanic techniques without necessarily taking on the role of shamanic practitioner. We can drum for ourselves and that might be all we need to do. As part of my three-year training in creative shamanism, one of our tasks was to journey on a regular basis to ask for information about our soul's purpose or calling. I would journey to ask questions like: "Who am I?" "What are my gifts?" and "How will I be working in the future?" I recorded all the insights from these journeys in one notebook and now have this as a reference guide for my future endeavours. I found the practice very useful and life-affirming and I still do it. If it appeals to you then give it a try.

Practitioner Skills

If you are already working as a reiki professional then you will know that each client session is an opportunity to hone your skills as a space-holder, therapist, guide, or teacher. The more you practise and experience reiki and the drum, the more confident and adventurous you become. Being a successful therapist or healer is an art, particularly in listening to what is present and trusting in your craft. Many essential practitioner skills can be learned and honed with practice. It's also imperative that you continue to address your own healing in order to hold a clear space for others, as has previously been discussed in detail.

When I first started to offer reiki professionally, I was painfully shy and felt awkward, which made it hard for me to gain rapport with my clients. I needed to work on my practitioner skills! Fortunately, self-practice together with confidence gained through experience helped me to overcome my insecurities and become a practitioner who clients feel safe with. Even if you only share reiki on friends, family, or colleagues, each time you offer reiki or play the drum you will be perfecting your craft. Below are some further pointers to help enhance your client work.

Diagnostic Journey

In Chapter 4 I guided you through a simple diagnostic exercise that you can perform for yourself or a client using the beat of the drum as an indicator of where in the body requires healing (see page 96). Drumming in this way is a simple diagnostic tool that helps you to interact with a client and gain their insight into what is needed, and also helps to build rapport. Another type of diagnostic can be undertaken before you even meet a client. This may be useful to help you tune in to the energy or the issue that you will be working on and also to ask whether or not you are the right practitioner to do this work.

The diagnostic journey is normally a short journey with your guide and the reiki symbols to help you connect with the client and the energies involved.

You undertake this journey after a client has booked a treatment with you and before you see them for the treatment itself.

The intention for the diagnostic journey is normally something like:

Show me what I need to know about working with this client or
Show me what healing is needed here for this client or
Show me what there is to learn about working with this client.

NOTE: The diagnostic journey is not a healing journey. It is simply a journey for research and information. It is not an opportunity to start healing without a client's permission.

Once you are confident to journey for yourself, start practising journeying like this for clients and observe how it helps you gain deeper insight into the treatment.

If you don't find this technique useful then experiment with other ways to gain insight into client treatments. You may prefer to sit in *gassho* meditation or connect with your spirit guides by other means. If you enjoy working with oracle cards, for example, you may find that tuning in and picking an oracle card to show you the energy behind the client session will be helpful information for you.

If you don't feel that a treatment with the client will be a positive experience or if something is revealed to you that you don't feel comfortable taking on, then refer your client to another practitioner.

Client Treatments and Getting to the Root of the Matter

I have found that the clearer the intention, the more focused the healing and guidance I can offer and the more beneficial it is for the client. Often our clients may not have thought that much about what they are seeking; they might be just following a nudge that has led them to reiki for some relaxation. This is wonderful and I feel that as energy workers, it's our role to gently ask further questions to help clients go a little deeper into the core of the issue so that we can truly help them make a change.

This example below highlights how this can result in a client admitting to themselves the real issue and can therefore help with getting closer to the root cause.

Client: "What's my intention? Oh, I just want to feel relaxed and receive healing."

Practitioner: "Is there anything specific that is making you feel stressed at the moment?"

Client: "Well, um, it's a busy time at work, I'm not getting on well with my boss, there have been some redundancies. I have a lot more on my plate than before and it's exhausting."

Practitioner: "Have you managed to speak to anyone about this? Is there any support that you can receive?"

Client: "I haven't had the confidence to put myself forward. The job I really want is in another department."

Practitioner: "Would it feel more helpful today if we were to rephrase your intention to give you specific assistance at work?"

Client: "Yes, that would help if it's possible."

Practitioner: "What do you think is needed at work? What would help you?"

Client: "Um, well I guess I'm shy, I just need the courage to speak up for what I want and ask my supervisor to put me forwards for a different role."

Practitioner: "How about we change 'to feel relaxed and receive healing' to 'to relax, trust myself and open to support at work'?"

Client: "Yes, thank you, that feels more specific."

This is an example of how asking a few more questions can narrow down an intention. This also helps clients realize what exactly it is that is bugging them. Often it takes a friendly ear and smile to coax this information out of their hearts. This example might even get more specific over time. Still using the example above, the next treatment might gently lead into helping the client become more confident in their abilities and knowing their true worth. Always make sure a client is happy with the intention and that it uses their words, not yours. By all means suggest words and phrases but make sure they repeat them and agree with them.

Guidance for Reiki Teachers and the Attunement Process

I find that due to its power and ability to connect, the drum naturally wants to weave its way into every aspect of my reiki practice. This includes the attunement process. As a reiki teacher, I have been taught a specific ritual for this sacred process but, over the years, this process has changed and I find that it is becoming more about holding and transmitting the frequency, rather than going through the complex routine of symbols that I have been taught. This, I feel, is the way that Usui intended. I find the drum a great facilitator in helping me to hold this high frequency, and so it is not uncommon for me to play the drum at the beginning or end of the attunement process for all levels of reiki.

When I am training students to work with the drum I also offer them an attunement that connects them to reiki, to their drum and also to me and the lineage that I carry. While I did receive an attunement during my reiki drum training, I have been intuitively guided to create my own process and this is different with each set of students as their energies are all individual. I do not wish to detail the process here, because I believe that if you feel guided to attune students to their drums then a process will be shown to you via your spirit helpers and reiki. However, here are some of the actions that are usually included in my drum attunement process:

- A ceremony to open the space, like that shown in Chapter 6; this will involve the students drumming too.
- A prayer inviting in all the drummers and reiki healers who have gone before us into the space.
- A meditation, while I drum, to help participants connect to their breath and bring awareness to the energy circuits in the body and activate their receiving channels.
- An invitation for students to hold their drums throughout the attunement process, in whatever way they are guided to do. I have seen students resting them face-up on their knees, hugging them to their hearts, or placing their hands very gently either side of the drum as it rests on its side.
- Drumming over the students through their energy field and over certain chakras.
- Students will feel the reverberation of the drum, not only in their energy field and physical body but also on their drum head.
- A welcome ritual after the student is attuned.
- A closing ceremony in which we all drum together to bring momentum to their path.

- Invitation for students to journal and reflect in quiet time following the process.

Drumming for Clients Recap

Throughout this book I've covered many different ways to incorporate the drum into client healing sessions as part of your reiki practice. To help you get started and avoid overwhelm, here's a summary.

Keep It Simple

- As a meditation tool to help clients relax or release.
- As a diagnostic tool with the client present – the client indicating where they sense the drum in their body or the practitioner using the drum to scan and sense the energy.
- As a healing tool: drum over the body as part of a hands-on reiki treatment for specific healing.
- As a distance healing tool with the client not physically present.
- As a background rhythm to aid relaxation or grounding or with guided visualization.
- As a healing tool for expression: offer the client a drum and unleash their rhythm.

Take It to Another Level

- As a diagnostic tool before the treatment. Undertake a diagnostic journey to sense the energy.
- As a remote healing tool for yourself, a client or a past situation during a shamanic journey in the shamanic realms.
- As a tool that takes the client on a journey so that they can find out specific information and discover the shamanic universe.
- As part of group healing circles.
- As part of a healing ceremony for individuals or for groups.
- As a tool to help a client connect with nature, plant spirits, elements or other places.
- For specific shamanic healing techniques like soul retrieval, psychopomp or extraction (beyond the scope of this book).
- For drumming attunements to help clients feel fully present with the spirit of their drum (and reiki).

Healing Animals

I'm often asked whether or not it's beneficial to use the drum with animals and your pets. My dogs have always been drawn to the drumbeat and enjoy lying down to receive; however, each animal will be different. It goes without saying that animals and birds are highly sensitive to sound and have the capacity to hear a wider range than we do, so be mindful. Experiment with a soft drumbeat about a metre away from the animal, and move yourself and shift your drumbeat accordingly depending on the animal's response.

TAKE ACTION Meeting Your Animal's Unseen Helpers

This is a lovely journey to practise with your pet. Hold your intention to connect with the animal's spirit helpers. You may wish to start by sending reiki to the animal to ensure they are calm, then pick up your drum and drum softly. Invite the animal's guides to reveal themselves to you. You may sense this in your heart and in the energy field. Find out what they can they tell you about this animal. When you feel ready, stop drumming and finish the session with more reiki to soothe the animal. Give thanks for the experience and the guidance you received and close your space. This method is like a diagnostic journey and helps you to glean information about how to help the animal, which can then inform further reiki healing or drum work.

TAKE A BEAT

The pace, depth and direction of your drum practice with reiki depends on your connection to your spirit guides and your personal experience. The more you connect and develop your relationship with guides and your drum through your own exploration of the shamanic journey, the more you expand your sense of knowing and trust. The opportunities for learning, growing and healing are as endless as your creativity and drive to reveal the truth. This work is spirit-led and flows through you at the pace that you are ready for. You are the channel; which is why it's essential to attend to your own healing. As you heal, the world around you transforms. You are an agent of change. You don't have to practise reiki or the drum professionally to be this change; shining your authentic nature into the world is enough. Trust in what the drumbeat and reiki guide you forward to create.

The Beat Goes On
Final Thoughts

With one hand on my drum and the other on my heart to receive, I sit here surrounded by the sounds of nature: the birdsong, the leaves rustling in the gentle breeze. In the background I can hear the traffic rumbling by; civilization does exist, yes life is really busy. There are things to do. But yet as I sit in this grove of trees, my feet firmly placed upon the Earth, my back straight, aligning the crown of my head up to the heavens. I can feel the presence of my drum in my heart opening to a deeper truth. The truth of who I am and how powerful we all are.

We each of us have a part to play, a voice that needs to sing and a rhythm to dance and weave. The animals, plants, elements and birds, they weave their magic too alongside us in the web of all things. The ancestors are whispering, your spirit guides are nudging you to step through the portal. You have reiki and the drum to keep you on your path, aligning with a fearless force of light that urges you forwards like a boat crashing through the waves.

As we play our drums together we create waves, we create a crescendo of love, compassion and connection that has the ability to move mountains, to recreate the world. It's time for this power to unfurl and it's time for you to dance to the drumbeat that is calling you forwards from your heart. You are the instrument that plays, your heartbeat is your drum.

In writing this book I have reviewed many of the drumming practices that are so familiar to me they have become second nature. I have been able to revisit some practices where, although I have moved away from them, I can still appreciate how useful they have been to me and will be for others. It has also reminded me how much the drum has helped shape my path as a healer, teacher, writer, partner and friend. It was also an opportunity to look over old journals, in which I found answers to questions that I was holding in my heart. Isn't it amazing how wise we truly are when we give ourselves the time and space to connect with our inner wisdom?

I hoped this book would make you want to pick up your drum, so please do! In writing it, I have certainly been saying to myself, "I need to drum more!"

I don't have all of the answers, but I do have a piece of the puzzle, and so do you. If you are still wondering, how does all this connect to reiki?, then ask that question as you drum. If you are still unsure about how to drum for a client, then pick up your drum and ask it to show you. If you are struggling with shamanic journeying with the drum, then release the pressure, drum with reiki to offer others healing or drum for joy instead, rather than with an intention to journey. There are a myriad of ways to journey into other realms for insight, if it appeals to you, you don't have to drum.

In fact, you don't have to drum at all. Reiki is simple, highly effective and a powerful tool for self-realization and for helping others heal themselves. I just have a feeling, though, that once you have picked up the drum, you won't be able to put it down.

When editing this book I took a final journey to ask what was needed for the energy of the book and those reading. Perhaps I was hoping for one more technique, a download with complexity that would make me appear clever and learned, or a lightning bolt of healing to blast away my insecurities. Instead – or rather, as usual – I experienced a very clear, consistent, heartfelt message. The guidance was actually just one simple word – community. This simultaneously came from deep within me and from outside of me in the energy field around me. I became alive with it in a flowing, dancing wave as golden and sweet as honey, only lighter, more fluid and free. We're not meant to drum alone. We're meant to join our heartbeats and drum together as a whole symphony of loving souls who hold the light and radiate a frequency of truth and love. This is community. This is the power of the drum.

*May the drum reach those parts of you that are
hidden and precious.*

*May it help your inner sound vibrate out loudly and
confidently into the world.*

*May it help you discover places, beings and deep wisdom
that you could only have imagined otherwise.*

*May it help you connect to your inner wisdom with a
renewed sense of certainty and trust.*

*May it help guide you along your reiki path in the
direction that you are meant to flow.*

*May it reveal those secrets that you have hidden
from yourself.*

*May it assist you in helping others experience the creative
forces of the universe for themselves.*

*May the drum feel connected, alive, vibrant and true
and may your voice sing out with love and change.
The song for change is ours to compose and sing together.*

*Deep blessings for your reiki practice and for the
beautiful sound of your drum and the music it makes
with the spirit of reiki within you.*

*Drum your dreams into being with your reiki hands
one beat at a time.*

Appendix

Shamanic Reiki
Journey Checklist

- Prepare your space
- Call in your guides and helpers (and reiki!)
- Prepare yourself
- Tune in to your intention and your motivation
- Invite a guide to be with you
- Drum or listen to a drumming track when you feel ready
- Self-treat with reiki (if listening to a drumming track)
- Relax and release judgement and expectation
- Allow the beat of the drum to take you on a journey
- Use the reiki symbols to help you make the connection
- Keep your focus on your intention
- Explore with curiosity and open all of your senses
- Let go of control
- Trust
- Ask questions
- Complete the journey and give thanks
- Ground yourself and integrate the experience
- Write down key points
- Close your space when you are done
- Make sure you act on any guidance given

Shamanic Journey Journal

Date:

Journey intention:

Journey method:

Feelings beforehand:

Feelings afterwards:

Journey specifics:

Guide(s) that I connected to:

Journey themes and feelings:

What feels significant about the journey?

Key message/guidance that I received:

In what way does the journey answer my intention?

How can I integrate this information/healing?

What further action can I take?

What has shifted (this can be added weeks, months or even years later)?:

Shamanic Reiki
Treatment Flow

Here's a reminder of the flow of a treatment.

Pre-session

- As soon as a session is booked, subtle energies will already be at work, so watch for dreams, signs, omens, synchronicities, unusual events, and ask the client to do so also.
- Ask your client to open their heart to what they are really seeking from the session. What is opening for them and what are they ready to leave behind?
- You could perform a diagnostic journey (see Chapter 8, page 181) to check in with your guides and feel the energy of the session to see what will be involved and check whether you are the right person to do this work.

Preparing for the Session

- Cleanse your space.
- Create the container.
- Connect with reiki and your guides (self-preparation).
- Make sure you are grounded and do a self-check-in: am I able to hold authority and compassion for this client?

Session (Pre-Treatment)

- Settle client in.
- Pre-treatment discussion with client as to what they are seeking – listen carefully.
- Find a clear intention.
- Explain the session and answer questions (explain shamanism and reiki, explain what to expect during the treatment, share the drum and how the treatment will complete).

During the Treatment

- Connect with reiki, your drum and guides, feel the safety of the container.
- Begin by using reiki to relax the client at first, raise vibrations of the energy field (5–10 mins).
- Do a short guided meditation (with or without the drum) if necessary to relax the client.
- Start your drumming (10–20 mins).
- Ask for guidance, allow spirit to move through you.
- Complete with more reiki (10–20 mins).
- Integration (Guidance may come here; maybe follow-up work like a ceremony, affirmation, creative project or time in nature is required).
- End the session as you would normally.

Post-Treatment and Feedback

- Disconnect from the client's energy once healing is complete.
- Make sure both you and the client are grounded. Offer the client water.
- Provide positive feedback and share any guidance received.
- Listen to your client share their experience if they wish.
- After-treatment care: what can you suggest to help the client integrate this healing? Where can you gently nudge the client to take action to increase their well-being?
- Make notes.
- Cleanse your energy and the space.
- Connect with nature.

Reiki Techniques

Gassho

Gassho in Japanese means "two hands coming together". The *gassho* meditation is a useful tool to use before you start a treatment. This gesture can be used as a mudra for meditation.

1. Sit quietly, keeping your spine as straight as possible.
2. Close your eyes and place your hands together in a prayer position – palm to palm – in front of your chest.
3. Breathe in through the nose and out through the mouth. Focus your attention on the point where the two middle fingers meet and forget everything else.

This is a simple meditation but will take practice. Try to relax as much as you can. As thoughts come into your mind, try not to give them any attention, just let them pass and bring your attention back to the point at which your fingers meet.

The Reiki Shower Technique

A quick and easy technique to activate and cleanse your energy body by flooding it with reiki like a shower of light. It is simple to incorporate at the same time as having a real (water) shower, or can be used whenever you wish to cleanse your energy body.

1. Sit quietly in *gassho* (prayer position) and focus effortlessly on your breath.
2. When you feel centred, connect to reiki with the intention that reiki flow to cleanse and activate your energy body.
3. Raise your hands above your head, making a bowl shape. For a few moments sense this bowl being filled with reiki. Your hands may even become tingly.

4. Then let your palms face downwards towards the crown of your head, and imagine reiki flowing out of them like a shower, flowing over and through your body cleansing and removing any negative energy.
5. Then bring your hands slowly down in front of your face and body, intending that the reiki should cleanse your energies and revitalize. Continue down to your feet.
6. Finally, turn your palms to face the floor and shake off any negative energy that flows out of your feet and into the Earth below, intending that it be transformed and used by the planet.
7. Repeat this exercise at least three times. You will feel cleansed, revitalized and more alive as reiki healing and light flows into all of your cells and fills every part of your body.
8. Afterwards, place your hands together again in *gassho* and spend a few moments experiencing gratitude for the reiki, and then finish – or, since reiki is activated and running through your whole body, this might be an ideal time to do some self-healing.

Joshin Kokyo Ho – Breathing Exercise to Focus the Mind and Purify the Spirit

This technique is part of the *Hatsurei Ho* technique, which helps magnify your energy. I like to use this part to focus my mind, feel centred and build energy.

1. Sit comfortably with your back straight and envisage drawing reiki energy in through your crown as you breathe in.
2. Pull the energy down from your crown into your *dantien* (a point a couple of fingers below your tummy button).
3. Keep the breath there for a few moments (do not strain).
4. Visualize the breath permeating your whole body and then exhale and imagine the breath/energy releasing through your hands, fingers, feet and toes, expanding out into your surroundings.
5. Begin the cycle again and find your own rhythm.
6. Repeat for as long as required and then place your hands in *gassho* and give thanks.

The *Kenyoku* Technique – Dry Bathing: Breathing Exercise to Purify the Spirit

Energy cleansing technique to help you detach from clients, thoughts and situations. Different Masters teach it in different ways; here is one variation.

Kenyoku can be done either with actual physical contact, or just off the surface of the body, in the aura.

1. Inhale through the nose and exhale through the mouth.
2. First, bring your *right* hand up to your *left* shoulder, the tips of your fingers at a point near where your collarbone ends, palm flat and facing the body.
   Move your hand diagonally down across your body from the *left* shoulder towards your *right* hip, in a smooth, measured, sweeping or brushing action. [In Hiroshi Doi's version of *Kenyoku*, you exhale with a "haa" sound as you do so.]
3. Next, bring your *left* hand up to your *right* shoulder, the tips of your fingers at a point near where your collarbone ends, palm flat and facing the body.
   Move your hand diagonally down across your body from the *right* shoulder towards your *left* hip, in a smooth, measured, sweeping or brushing action. [In Hiroshi Doi's version of *Kenyoku*, you exhale with a "haa" sound as you do so.]
4. Repeat this sequence once more with the right hand.
5. Now, place your right hand at the *edge* of your left shoulder – with left arm held straight out in front of you, palm up – move your hand along the outside of your left arm and down over the end of the fingers; repeat this with the left hand on the right arm; finish by repeating with right hand on left arm.

List of Exercises

❀ ❀ ❀ ❀

This is a list of all the Take Action points, self-reflections, and visualizations throughout the book.

Recommended Books

Reiki, Healing, and Energy Work

Eden, Donna and Feinstein, David. *Energy Medicine: How to use your body's energies for optimum health and vitality*. London, UK: Piatkus, 2008.

Emoto, Masuru. *The Hidden Messages in Water*. London, UK: Pocket Books, 2005.

Goldman, Jonathan. *The 7 Secrets of Sound Healing*. London, UK: Hay House, 2008.

———. *Healing Sounds: The Power of Harmonics*. Rochester, VT: Healing Arts Press, 2022.

Hamilton, David. *Why Woo Woo Works*. London, UK: Hay House, 2021.

Johnstone, Fay. *Plant Spirit Reiki: Energy Healing with the Elements of Nature*. Rochester, VT: Findhorn Press, 2020.

Lubeck, Petter and Rand. *The Spirit of Reiki: The Complete Handbook of the Reiki System*. Varanasi, India: Pilgrims Publishing, 2001.

Meacham, Elizabeth. *Earth Spirit Dreaming: Shamanic Ecotherapy Practices*. Rochester, VT: Findhorn Press, 2020.

McTaggart, Lynne. *The Field: The Quest for the Secret Force of the Universe*. London, UK: Element, 2003.

PathFinder Ewing, Jim. *Reiki Shamanism*. Rochester, VT: Findhorn Press, 2008.

Pearson, Nicholas. *Foundations of Reiki Ryoho: A Manual of Shoden and Okuden*. Rochester, VT: Healing Arts Press, 2018.

Quest, Penelope. *Reiki for Life: The Complete Guide to Reiki Practice for Levels 1, 2 & 3*. New York: TarcherPerigee, 2016.

Rowland, Amy. *Intuitive Reiki for Our Times: Essential Techniques for Enhancing Your Practice*. Rochester, VT: Healing Arts Press, 2006.

Steine, Bronwen and Steine, Frans. *The Reiki Sourcebook*. Hants, UK: O Books, 2010.

Shamanism

Blacker, Carmen. *The Catalpa Bow: A Study of Shamanistic Practices in Japan.* London, UK: Routledge, 1999.

Day, Carol. *Drum: The Rhythm of Shamanism.* Fife, UK: Independent Publishing Network, 2018.

——. *Shamanic Dreaming: Connecting with Your Inner Visionary.* Rochester, VT: Findhorn Press, 2023.

Farmer, Steven. *Animal Spirit Guides: An Easy-to-Use Handbook for Identifying and Understanding Your Power Animals and Animal Spirit Helpers.* London, UK: Hay House, 2022.

Ingerman, Sandra. *Shamanic Journeying: A Beginner's Guide.* Boulder, CO: Sounds True Inc., 2008.

——. *Walking in Light: The Everyday Empowerment of a Shamanic Life.* Boulder, CO: Sounds True Inc., 2015.

Ingerman, Sandra and Wesselman, Hank. *Awakening to the Spirit World: The Shamanic Path of Direct Revelation.* Boulder, CO: Sounds True Inc., 2010.

Redmond, Layne. *When the Drummers Were Women.* Vermont, VT: Echo Point Books & Media, 2018.

Acknowledgements

W hat a blessing it is to write a third book. I am humbled by how influential reiki continues to be on my path and feel deeply grateful for the lineage of healers and teachers that I am part of and which has helped bring the light of reiki energy out into the world. Specific thanks go to my two reiki teachers Tripuri Dunne and Keri Manning-Dedman, and to Sarah Gregg for introducing me to reiki drum all those years ago and placing my first drum in my hands! Heartfelt thanks also to Rebekah Arthurs for having so much patience with me when I first learned how to journey and to both Nova Poirier and Carol Day, two of my shamanic teachers spanning the globe who have empowered me with the tools that I need to transform myself as I walk this incredible path.

I feel deeply blessed to have learned from those teachers together with all of my students and peers who I have shared with and received insights from in the safe container of sacred circles over the years. I feel deeply thankful to everyone who has drummed with me and the team of helping spirits that continue to nudge me forwards. If it wasn't for that dream, I wouldn't have sent the book proposal to Findhorn Press!

When I drum I feel the presence of all the women who were once drummers across the world and I feel honoured and grateful to be continuing the drumbeats in the rhythm that they first created. Last but not least gratitude to my husband, my friends and family who act as my cheerleaders always. Blessed be!

About the Author

Photo by Becky Henderson

Fay Johnstone combines more than twenty years of reiki practice with elemental qigong, plant medicine, and creative shamanism to bring the healing power of nature to assist us with our personal transformation. As well as studying herbal medicine, she ran an organic flower and herb farm in Nova Scotia for some years before returning to her native Scotland. The path of the drum and reiki led Fay to connect even more deeply with nature and plants. The author of *Plant Spirit Reiki* and *Plants That Speak, Souls That Sing,* Fay offers training and retreats from her garden in Fife, Scotland.

For more information please visit **www.fayjohnstone.com**.

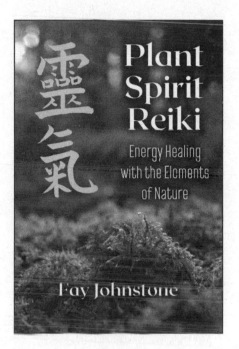

Plant Spirit Reiki

by Fay Johnstone

A PRACTICAL WORKBOOK for energy healers and reiki practitioners that shows how to partner with plant spirit allies and the forces of nature for powerful healing for yourself, others, and our planet. Includes many simple exercises, meditations, and reiki practices to help you intuitively work with plants as part of your reiki practice.

978-1-64411-104-8

Plant That Speaks, Souls That Sing
by Fay Johnstone

ENGAGE WITH THE INTELLIGENCE of nature to discover your unique role and deepen your spiritual path on Earth. This practical guide to plant consciousness includes more than 40 simple exercises, shamanic journeys, and meditations to guide you on a heart-centred journey of transformation as you commune with the environment, the seasons, the moon, plant spirits, and the Earth Heart.

978-1-84409-751-7